Cooking Alaska's Wild Halibut

By Kathy Doogan

Illustrations by Ray Troll

Anchorage

Cooking Alaska's Wild Halibut

© 2010 by Alaska Cook Book Co.

All rights reserved. This book may not be reproduced in whole or in part without the written permission of the publisher.

Distributed by

Todd Communications
611 E. 12th Ave., Suite 102
Anchorage, Alaska 99501-4603 U.S.A.
Telephone: (907) 274-TODD (8633)
Telefax: (907) 929-5550
Sales@toddcom.com
WWW.ALASKABOOKSANDCALENDARS.COM

With other offices and warehouses in:
Ketchikan, Juneau, Fairbanks and Nome, Alaska

**Written, edited and designed by
Kathy Doogan / Raven Design**

Artwork © Ray Troll, 2010

First Printing December, 2010
10 9 8 7 6 5 4 3 2 1

ISBN: 978-1-57833-503-9

Printed by Everbest Printing Co., Ltd., Nansha, China
through **Alaska Print Brokers**, Anchorage, Alaska.

Additional copies of this book or *Cooking Alaska's Wild Salmon*
may be ordered directly from the distributor
for US $19.95 each (includes US $6.00 postage & handling).

On the cover: *Hooked on Halibut*, from Sitka's Wild Fish Mural, © Ray Troll, 2005

Contents

Acknowledgements 4

Introduction 6

Appetizers & Salads 10

Soups & Stews 22

Main Courses 32

Sauces, Marinades & Embellishments 86

Recipe Index 94

Acknowledgements

For their indispensible help in creating this book, my heart-felt thanks go to my dear friends who conscientiously tested the recipes: Krissy Gable, Cass Crandall, RuthAnn Dickie, Heather Beaty, Davida Kapler, Katie Koester, Rosanne Pagano, Barbara Doogan, Susan Sullivan, Tina Seaton, and Kayla Epstein. They gave me countless suggestions and comments that ultimately made the recipes better, and have my sincere gratitude.

Many thanks also go to Ray Troll, whose whimsical artwork has added so much to the pages of this book; and to the talented chefs from around Alaska who generously shared their best halibut recipes: Brett Custer, The Homestead Restaurant (Homer); Dali Frazier, Wasabi's (Homer); Jens Hansen, Jens' Restaurant (Anchorage); Patrick Hoogerhyde, Glacier Brewhouse (Anchorage); Brett Knipmeyer, Kinley's Restaurant (Anchorage); Collette Nelson, Ludvig's Bistro (Sitka); Justin Persons, The Double Musky Inn (Girdwood); George Pitsilionis, Paradiso's Restaurant (Kenai); and Tim Allen who shared a recipe created by chef Leslie Simutis of Ray's Waterfront (Seward)

Finally, I'd like to thank my husband, Mike, who inspires me to cook and who always helps keep me on course.

— *Kathy Doogan*

Introduction

Wild Alaska Halibut

The deep, cold waters off Alaska are home to the largest of all flatfishes – wild Alaska halibut. Although they commonly weigh in at up to 100 pounds, individual Alaska halibut have reached record weights of more than 400 pounds and lengths over eight feet. Halibut are born and spend most of their lives in deep water, feeding on all kinds of other fish and even shellfish. They live up to 40 years, with the females typically living longer than males.

Halibut are possibly best known for their unusual growth pattern. From the time they hatch until the age of about 6 months, halibut look like any other fish, with one eye on each side of their head. But then they change — one eye migrates so they end up with both eyes on the top of their head and their body flattens out into a typical flatfish shape.

Halibut are at the center of a lucrative commercial fishery in Alaska. In the past, the commercial halibut fishery was operated like a competition, with specified "openings," periods of one to two days when all fishermen participated in a race to catch as many fish as they could. This system has been discontinued because unpredictable weather conditions during the opening periods caused safety issues and the short periods of availability of halibut in markets affected prices. Today the fishery uses an individual fishing quota (IFQ) system under which the IFQ holder is allowed to take a specified amount of fish at any time during the open fishing season, typically from February to November.

Currently, the only legal method for commercially catching halibut is with longlines, heavy fishing lines with baited hooks at regular

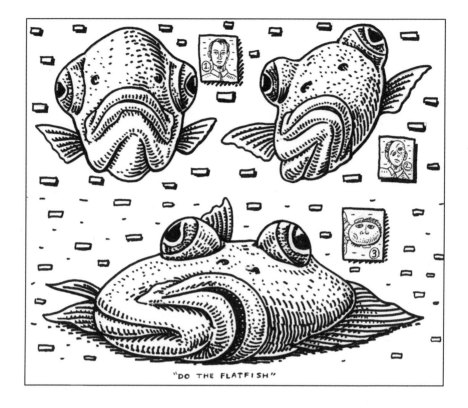
"DO THE FLATFISH"

intervals, which are laid on the ocean floor. The lines are left for several hours or up to a day before being pulled in.

A vibrant sport fishery also revolves around wild Alaska halibut. In addition to personal fishing and the numerous fishing charters that are available, fishermen can participate in one of the many fishing derbies held in coastal communities throughout the state. One of the better known contests, the Homer Jackpot Halibut Derby, rewards the angler who catches the largest fish of the season with a prize that can exceed $50,000.

Nutritional Information

Because it is low in fat and high in protein and has a mild, clean flavor, wild Alaska halibut is a favorite of health-conscious consumers and cooks — a mere three ounce portion contains only about 120 calories and less than three grams of fat, yet it provides

Introduction

22 grams of protein. Halibut's dense, firm flesh lends itself to a variety of cooking methods, from roasting to pan frying to grilling, and the mild meat is a perfect platform for an endless variety of sauces, marinades and other added flavors.

Notes on the Recipes in this Book

Most of the recipes in this book call for halibut fillets (usually skinless) rather than halibut steaks. If only halibut steaks are available, you can trim the skin off or you can cook the steaks with the skin on and easily peel it off when it's done. If it is appropriate to the recipe (for example, if you are simply baking the fish in the oven), you can use the same approach for fillets — cook the fish and the skin will slip off easily. But removing the skin from raw fillets is another matter. Unless you've done it many times, it can be a little tricky. The easiest way to do it is to ask your butcher to remove the skin for you. If that's not an option, search "removing halibut skin" on the internet — you'll find many videos showing you how to do it yourself.

For simplicity and even cooking, buy halibut fillets, steaks or cheeks of the same thickness. The key to succulent halibut is to know when it's done — overcooked fish, just like meat, can be dry and tough. Halibut is done when you can easily pull the flakes of flesh apart with a fork, or when the meat is opaque all the way through. When in doubt, it is better to remove the fish from heat a bit before it is done; residual heat will continue to cook it a few minutes longer.

— Kathy Doogan

Appetizers & Salads

Bacon-Wrapped Halibut Pops

    4 slices bacon (not thick-sliced)
    1 pound skinless halibut fillet, 3/4" to 1" thick
    3 tablespoons bottled teriyaki sauce OR barbeque sauce, plus extra for dipping if desired

Preheat oven to 400°.

Cut each slice of bacon lengthwise into 3 narrow strips, then cut each strip in half crosswise; you should have 24 pieces of bacon approximately 1/2" by 4" to 5".

Cut halibut into 24 cubes as equal in size as possible. Place cubes in a bowl and toss to coat them lightly with teriyaki or barbeque sauce. Wrap one piece of bacon snugly around each fish cube and secure with a toothpick. Place halibut pops on a lightly-greased baking sheet and bake for 8 to 10 minutes, until halibut is opaque and bacon is beginning to turn brown and crisp. Serve with additional teriyaki or barbeque sauce for dipping, if desired.

Makes 24 appetizers

Halibut Cocktail Kebabs

>20 to 24 bamboo cocktail skewers, at least 6" long
>1/2 cup olive oil
>2 tablespoons balsamic vinegar
>1 teaspoon Dijon mustard
>2 cloves garlic, minced or pressed
>1 pinch red pepper flakes
>1 teaspoon sugar
>1/2 teaspoon salt
>1 pound halibut fillet, cut into 1" cubes
>1 medium zucchini, cut into quarters then into 1" pieces
>10 to 12 cherry tomatoes, cut in half

Place oven rack about 6" from heat source and preheat broiler to high. Soak bamboo skewers in a dish of water for at least 30 minutes before using.

In a small bowl, whisk together olive oil, vinegar, mustard, garlic, red pepper flakes, sugar and salt. Pour into a large zip-top plastic bag. Add halibut cubes, zucchini pieces and whole cherry tomatoes. Turn bag to coat everything well, then seal and allow fish and vegetables to marinate at room temperature for at least 20 minutes but no longer than 30 minutes.

Drain and discard marinade from bag. Onto each skewer, thread 1 piece of zucchini, 1 halibut cube and 1 cherry tomato half. Place skewers on a rack over a baking sheet. Broil for 5 to 6 minutes, turning once, until halibut is cooked through.

Makes about 20 appetizers

Appetizers

Halibut Nacho Bites

1/2 cup mayonnaise, bottled or homemade (recipe on page 88)
1 teaspoon chili powder
1 cup peanut oil or other vegetable oil (for frying)
1/2 cup flour
1/2 teaspoon salt
Pinch of black pepper
1 egg, beaten
1/2 to 3/4 cup Panko (Japanese-style bread crumbs)
1 pound skinless halibut, cut into 3/4" to 1" cubes
Tortilla chips
1 cup chopped iceberge lettuce
1 cup bottled salsa (mild or spicy, according to taste)

In a small bowl, combine mayonnaise and chili powder. Refrigerate until ready to assemble Nacho Bites.

Heat oil in a large non-stick skillet over medium-high heat. Place flour in a flat bowl or pie plate; stir in salt and pepper. Place beaten egg and bread crumbs in two additional bowls or pie plates. Dip fish cubes into flour, then into egg and finally into bread crumbs, coating well. Use tongs to place the coated fish cubes into the hot oil. Cook over medium heat, turning to brown all sides, until fish is just done, about 3 or 4 minutes total. Remove fish to paper towels to drain.

To assemble Nacho Bites: Spread tortilla chips in a single layer on a large plate. On each chip, place a small mound of lettuce and a teaspoon or so of salsa. Place a cooked halibut cube on the salsa, then top the halibut with a small dollop of chili mayonnaise. Serve immediately.

Makes about 30 appetizers

Mini Halibut Cakes

   2 slices stale white bread (or substitute 3/4 cup packaged bread crumbs)
   2 cups cooked halibut (about 1 pound)
   1/4 teaspoon salt
   1 pinch to 1/4 teaspoon cayenne pepper, according to taste
   1/2 teaspoon seafood seasoning, such as Old Bay®
   2 large eggs
   3 tablespoons mayonnaise, bottled or homemade (see recipe on page 88)
   1 large green onion, white and green part, finely chopped (about 2 tablespoons)
   1 small rib of celery, finely diced (about 2 tablespoons)
   1 tablespoon butter
   2 tablespoons vegetable oil

Tear bread into pieces and process in food processor or blender to make coarse crumbs; set aside.

In a medium bowl, flake halibut with a fork. Add 1/4 cup of the bread crumbs, salt, cayenne, egg, mayonnaise and green onion. Mix until all ingredients are combined. (Recipe can be made ahead to this point; cover halibut mixture and refrigerate for no more than one day; store remaining crumbs in a zip top bag until ready to use.)

Heat butter and oil over medium high heat in a non-stick skillet. Spread reserved crumbs on a plate. Drop halibut mixture by rounded tablespoonfuls onto crumbs; turn over and pat to flatten slightly. Carefully place halibut cakes in skillet and cook, turning once, until golden brown, about 1 minute per side. Remove to paper towels to drain.

Serve warm with cocktail or tartar sauce (see recipe on page 89).

Makes about 30 appetizers

Wasabi's Hot-Butt Dip

Chef Dali Frazier
Wasabi's Restaurant, Homer

2 pounds fresh halibut fillet, cut into 1" cubes
3/4 cup mayonnaise
1/2 cup sour cream
Juice of 1 lemon
2 green jalapeno peppers, roasted and finely chopped
  (remove seeds for less heat)
1/2 cup shredded parmesan cheese
1/2 cup shredded mozzarella cheese
1/2 cup finely chopped green onions
1/2 cup finely chopped artichoke hearts (canned or frozen)
1 teaspoon garlic powder
1 teaspoon paprika
1 teaspoon onion powder
Salt and pepper to taste
Crostini (see **Note**)

Preheat oven to 375°.

Combine all ingredients in a large bowl. Pour into an ovenproof dish and bake for 20 to 25 minutes, until browned and bubbly. Serve hot with crostini.

Note: You can purchase ready-made crostini or make your own: Preheat oven to 375°. Cut a french bread baguette into 1/2" slices. Drizzle both sides of bread slices with a small amount of olive oil and arrange them on a sheet pan. Bake until light brown and crisp, about 5 minutes total (turn slices over about halfway through baking). Remove pan from oven and let crostini cool on a rack until ready to use.

Pickled Halibut

This recipe was given to me by my friend, Susan Sullivan. She notes that the halibut cooks best if it is at room temperature when you begin, and that cooling the completed mixture quickly will help to keep the halibut chunks intact.

    1 cup water
    1/3 cup dry white wine
    1 cup white vinegar
    1 tablespoon olive oil
    1/4 cup sugar
    2 teaspoons salt
    4 whole cloves
    10 peppercorns
    2 bay leaves
    2 pounds halibut (skin and bones removed), cut into
        1" cubes, at room temperature
    1 medium white onion, sliced thin
    1 lemon, sliced thin

In a capacious pot, combine all brine ingredients (water through bay leaves); bring to a fast boil, then cover pot and reduce to a slow simmer for 15 minutes.

Return brine to a full boil and put halibut into pot. Reduce heat and allow to simmer gently for 2 to 3 minutes, or until fish just barely flakes with a fork. Take pot off heat and, using a slotted spoon, remove the halibut from the hot brine. Spread fish on a plate or baking sheet to cool slightly. Strain brine through a fine sieve or cheesecloth-lined colander into a bowl. Place brine in refrigerator or freezer (cover pot to keep steam in) to cool down while completing the next step.

In the bottom of a chilled glass bowl (or large jar), place a layer of 1/3 of the onion and lemon slices then top with 1/3 of the halibut. Continue with 2 more layers, ending with halibut. Cover the fish with the cooled brine and refrigerate immediately.

Refrigerated and tightly covered, this treat will keep for weeks.

Appetizers

Island-Style Halibut Salad

1 cup plus 2 tablespoons orange juice, divided
1 tablespoon vegetable oil
1 tablespoon soy sauce
1 tablespoon rum (preferably dark)
1/2 teaspoon black pepper
3/4 pound to 1 pound skinless halibut fillet, cut into 1" chunks
1/4 cup olive oil
2 tablespoons rice vinegar
1/2 teaspoon orange zest (orange part only)
1/2 teaspoon sugar
Salt and pepper
1 large head of romaine, trimmed, washed and crisped
1 medium mango, peeled and cut into 1/2" cubes (see **Note**)
1 medium avocado, peeled and cut into 1/2" cubes
1 large rib of celery, thinly sliced on the diagonal
1/4 cup coarsely chopped macadamia nuts

Combine 1 cup orange juice, vegetable oil, soy sauce, rum and pepper in a bowl. Add the halibut chunks, stir to coat well and let marinate at room temperature about 15 to 20 minutes. Place the halibut and the marinade in a skillet over medium-low heat. Cover and cook, gently stirring occasionally to be sure fish does not stick, until the halibut is just done (check often to avoid overcooking). Using a slotted spoon, remove the halibut chunks carefully to a plate (discard cooking liquid) and chill in the refrigerator while you prepare the salad.

In a small bowl, whisk together the olive oil, remaining 2 tablespoons orange juice, rice vinegar, orange zest and sugar. Season with salt and pepper to taste and set dressing aside.

Cut or tear romaine into bite-sized pieces and place in a large salad bowl. Add mango, avocado, celery, macadamias and chilled halibut chunks. Pour dressing over and toss gently.

Serves 4

Note: If fresh mango is not available, you can substitute about 1 1/2 cups frozen mango chunks, thawed, or dice up some bottled mango spears (often available in the produce section of your supermarket).

Halibut and Avocado Salad

    1/2 pound cooked halibut (skin removed), broken or cut into bite-sized pieces
    1/4 cup olive oil
    2 tablespoons rice vinegar
    1/2 teaspoon sugar
    Salt and pepper
    4 cups mixed salad greens
    1 mango, peeled and cut into 1/2" cubes
    1 avocado, peeled and cut into 1/2" cubes
    1 small bell pepper (any color), cut into 1/4" cubes
    1 cup corn kernels (fresh or frozen, thawed)
    3 strips lean bacon, fried crisp, drained and crumbled
    1 tablespoon sesame or sunflower seeds (optional)

Use leftover halibut or steam or poach fish according to instructions on page 34. Chill halibut before assembling salad.

Prepare dressing by whisking together olive oil, vinegar, sugar and salt and pepper to taste. Toss halibut with about 1 tablespoon of the dressing and set remainder aside.

In a large salad bowl, toss greens, mango, avocado, bell pepper, corn kernels and bacon with remaining dressing until well mixed. Add halibut pieces and toss gently once or twice, just to distribute fish. Serve well chilled, sprinkled with sesame or sunflower seeds, if desired.

Serves 2

Appetizers

Tropical Halibut and Black Bean Salad

    1/4 cup olive oil
    1 tablespoons fresh-squeezed lime juice
    1 tablespoon balsamic vinegar
    1/2 teaspoon chili powder
    1/4 teaspoon salt
    1/8 teaspoon black pepper
    6 to 8 cups mixed salad greens
    1 can (15 ounces) black beans, rinsed and drained
    1 cup fresh or frozen (thawed) corn kernels
    1 1/2 cups fresh papaya or pineapple, peeled and cut into
        1/2" dice (see **Note**)
    1/4 cup red onion, diced, rinsed in cold water and drained
    1 pound cooked halibut fillet, broken into pieces (use
        leftover halibut or cook according to one of the basic
        recipes on page 34 and chill before proceeding)

Combine olive oil, lime juice, vinegar, chili powder, salt and pepper in a small bowl and set aside.

Place greens, black beans, corn, papaya or pineapple and onion in a large salad bowl. Pour dressing over and toss to mix well. Top with halibut chunks and toss gently just to mix in. Chill until ready to serve.

Serves 4

Note: If fresh papaya or pineapple are not available, you can substitute the same amount of canned pineapple chunks or canned mandarin orange segments.

Double Musky Halibut Ceviche

Chef Justin Persons
Double Musky Inn, Girdwood

Make this recipe a few hours or even a day in advance to allow the flavors to marry. At the Musky, they serve the Halibut Ceviche in an avocado half on top of a bed of romaine, but it is excellent as a dip with chips as well.

Halibut

    10 ounces halibut fillet, skin removed
    1/2 cup lemon juice
    1/2 cup sweetened lime juice (such as Rose's®)

Salad Mix

    1/4 cup olive oil
    1/4 cup ketchup
    6 ounces tomato juice
    1 teaspoon hot pepper sauce
    1 teaspoon salt
    1/2 teaspoon dried basil
    1/2 teaspoon dried oregano
    1 tablespoon fresh cilantro, minced
    1/2 cup bell peppers, diced
    1/2 cup onions, diced
    1 1/2 cups tomatoes, diced
    5 green olives, sliced
    1/2 cup black olives, sliced
    1/2 cup mushrooms, sliced

Trim any fat from the Halibut and dice into 1/2" cubes. Put the diced halibut into a small glass or stainless steel container (avoid aluminum) and add the lemon juice and sweetened lime juice. Stir the halibut together with the juices, making sure the fish is submerged in the liquid. Cover and refrigerate for three hours. (The acids in the juice will "cook" the halibut.)

Recipes From Alaska's Best Chefs

After 3 hours, check to see if the halibut is done by pulling apart a piece to see if it is opaque in the center. If the halibut is done, drain; if it's not done, continue to marinate a while longer then check again for doneness.

While the halibut is marinating, prepare the salad. In a medium bowl, stir together the olive oil, ketchup, tomato juice, hot pepper sauce, salt and herbs. Add the remaining ingredients and mix them together. Cover and refrigerate the salad mix until the halibut is done.

Finishing the ceviche: Drain the "cooked" halibut and stir it into the salad mix.

Serves 5

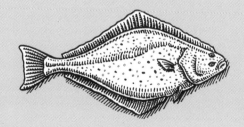

Soups & Stews

Halibut Chowder

    3 slices bacon, cut into 1/2" pieces
    2 tablespoons butter
    1 pound red or Yukon Gold potatoes (3 medium), peeled and cut into 1/2" cubes
    1 medium yellow onion, chopped
    1 teaspoon fresh thyme leaves (or 1/2 teaspoon dried thyme)
    1/4 cup flour
    2 cups whole milk
    1 cup half and half
    1 cup chicken broth
    Salt and pepper to taste
    1 pound halibut fillet, cut into 1" cubes

Heat a Dutch oven or medium-sized soup pot over medium heat. Add bacon and cook until browned and beginning to crisp; remove with a slotted spoon to drain on paper towels. Pour off all but 1 tablespoon of bacon drippings. Add butter, potatoes, onion and thyme and cook over medium heat, stirring often until onions are soft and potatoes are almost tender, about 10 minutes. Sprinkle in flour and cook, stirring constantly, for about 2 minutes.

Pour in milk, half and half and chicken broth, stir to mix well. Reduce heat and simmer, stirring often, until soup is thickened and potatoes are just cooked through (test with a fork). Taste and season with salt and pepper if necessary. Add halibut chunks and cooked bacon and continue simmering until halibut is just done, about 5 minutes.

Serves 4

White Halibut Chili

    2 tablespoons olive oil
    1 large yellow onion, chopped
    1 can (4 ounces) diced green chiles, mild or hot (according to taste), drained
    2 teaspoons cumin
    1 teaspoon dried oregano
    1 to 2 teaspoons chili powder, according to taste
    3 cups chicken broth
    3 cans (15 ounces) white beans, drained and rinsed
    Salt and pepper to taste
    1 pound skinless halibut fillet, cut into 1" cubes
    1/4 cup sour cream
    1/2 cup shredded Monterey Jack or Cheddar cheese
    Chopped cilantro

Heat the oil in a medium dutch oven or large saucepan. Add the onion and cook over medium-high heat, stirring often, until translucent (about 4 to 5 minutes). Stir in the green chilis, cumin, oregano and chili powder and cook for an additional minute or two. Add the chicken broth and the beans. Lower the heat, cover and simmer for about 20 minutes.

Remove about 1 cup of the beans to a medium bowl. Using a fork, mash the beans with about 1/4 cup of the cooking liquid until they form a fairly smooth paste (add more cooking liquid if necessary). Return mixture to pot and stir in well to thicken the chili. Taste and season with salt, pepper and more chili powder if needed.

Add the halibut chunks to the chili and stir gently. Cover pot and cook on low heat for 4 to 5 minutes or until halibut just flakes with a fork. (Do not over-stir or fish will break up.)

Ladle chili into bowls and top each with about 1 tablespoon of sour cream and a sprinkling of shredded cheese and chopped cilantro.

Serves 4

Soups & Stews

Easy Halibut Posole

Preparing classic posole (made with slow-cooked pork or chicken) can be a time-consuming proposition. This streamlined, non-traditional version can be on the table in less than an hour.

> 2 tablespoons vegetable oil
> 1 large white onion, diced (about 1 cup)
> 1 small jalapeno, chopped (optional, remove seeds for less heat)
> 3 cloves garlic, minced or pressed
> 2 cans (6 ounces each) whole green chiles, mild or hot (according to taste), drained
> 1 cup fresh cilantro (discard large stems)
> 1 teaspoon dried oregano
> 2 cans (15 ounces each) hominy, drained
> 4 cups chicken broth
> Salt and freshly ground pepper
> 1 pound skinless halibut fillet, cut into 1" chunks
> Assorted accompaniments (see below)

Heat the vegetable oil in a large saucepan over medium heat. Add the onion, jalapeno and garlic and cook until soft, about 4 minutes. Transfer to a blender, then add the drained chiles, cilantro, oregano and 1/2 cup of the drained hominy and purée until smooth. Return mixture to the saucepan and cook over medium heat, stirring until it thickens slightly, about 5 minutes.

Add the remaining hominy and the broth to the saucepan. Lower the heat and simmer for about 10 minutes. Taste soup and season with salt and pepper if needed. Stir in the halibut chunks, turn off the heat, cover and let stand, stirring gently once or twice, until halibut is just cooked through, about 10 minutes. Serve with any or all of the traditional accompaniments listed below.

Serves 4

Traditional accompaniments for posole include:

Shredded lettuce	Lime wedges
Chopped red onions	Chopped cilantro
Sour cream	Diced avocado
Toasted pumpkin seeds	Tortilla chips

Hot and Sour Halibut Soup

> 6 medium fresh shiitake mushrooms or 6 dried Chinese black mushrooms (available in Asian markets)
> 4 cups chicken broth
> 4 ounces firm tofu, cut into 1/2" cubes (optional, see **Note**)
> 1 can (8 ounces) bamboo shoots, rinsed, drained and cut into thin slices or matchsticks
> 2 tablespoons or more rice vinegar
> 2 tablespoons soy sauce
> 1 tablespoon cornstarch mixed with 1/4 cup water
> 1 teaspoon sugar
> 1 egg, beaten
> 1 teaspoon or more ground white pepper (do not substitute black pepper)
> 1 teaspoon sesame oil
> 2 large green onions, white and green parts thinly sliced
> 1/2 pound (about 1 to 1 1/2 cups) cooked halibut, skin and bones removed
> Salt to taste
> Chili oil (for serving, optional)

Cut tough stems from mushrooms and thinly slice the caps. (If using dried mushrooms, soak them in warm water to cover for 20 to 30 minutes before draining and slicing.)

Place chicken broth, sliced mushrooms, tofu, bamboo shoots, vinegar, soy sauce, cornstarch mixture and sugar in a large pot. Bring to a boil over high heat; cook for 1 to 2 minutes, until thickened. Turn off heat and slowly stir in beaten egg, using a fork to break it up into strands as it cooks.

Break halibut into small pieces and gently stir it into the hot soup with the white pepper, sesame oil and green onions. Taste and adjust vinegar, white pepper and salt to taste, then serve immediately. Pass chili oil at the table if desired for more heat.

Serves 4

Note: Tofu is a traditional ingredient in hot and sour soup but if you don't like it you can leave it out.

Ludvig's Thai Halibut Soup

Chef Colette Nelson
Ludvig's Bistro, Sitka

This recipe was inspired by Chef Nelson's friend, Dwang.

- 1/2 cup cilantro, chopped
- 1/2 cup lemon grass, chopped
- 1/2 cup scallions, thinly sliced
- 1/2 cup basil, chopped
- 1/4 cup garlic, chopped
- 1/4 cup ginger, chopped
- 4 roma tomatoes, diced
- 1 teaspoon red pepper flakes (more or less to taste)
- 1 cup fresh lime juice, divided
- 1 cup soy sauce, divided
- 2 pounds halibut fillet, cut into 1" cubes
- 2 large yellow onions, diced
- 2 cups button mushrooms
- 3 tablespoons vegetable oil
- 2 cans coconut milk (not "lite")
- 5 cups vegetable stock
- 1/4 cup fish sauce
- 1 teaspoon Thai red curry paste (more or less to taste)
- 1/2 cup raw sugar
- Lime wedges, chopped basil and cilantro (for serving)

Prepare marinade by combining cilantro, lemon grass, scallions, basil, garlic, ginger, tomatoes, red pepper flakes, 1/2 cup lime juice and 1/2 cup soy sauce in a large zip-top plastic bag. Add halibut, seal bag and refrigerate while proceeding.

In a soup pot, saute the onions and mushrooms in oil until soft. Add the coconut milk, vegetable stock, fish sauce, Thai curry paste, sugar and remaining 1/2 cup lime juice and 1/2 cup soy sauce; mix well. Bring to a boil, reduce heat and add the halibut and marinade. Stir gently once or twice. Remove from heat, cover and let stand until halibut is cooked through. Serve with lime wedges and chopped basil and cilantro.

Vietnamese Halibut Soup

    4 cups low-sodium chicken broth or vegetable broth
    1 tablespoon Vietnamese fish sauce (optional)
    1 tablespoon soy sauce
    1 clove garlic, minced or pressed
    1 teaspoon ground coriander
    1/2 teaspoon black pepper
    2 whole star anise OR 1 teaspoon five spice powder
    6 whole cloves
    1 inch piece of fresh ginger, peeled and thinly sliced
    1 pound halibut fillet (with skin on), cut into 4 portions
    4 large green onions, thinly sliced
    2 to 3 cups cooked rice noodles (prepare according to package directions)
    1 cup bean sprouts
    1/2 cup fresh basil leaves (for serving)
    1 small jalapeno or other hot pepper, sliced (for serving)
    4 lime wedges (for serving)
    Chili oil (for serving)

Prepare broth: In a large sauce pan or small stockpot, combine broth, fish sauce, soy sauce, garlic, coriander, pepper, star anise (or five spice powder), cloves and ginger over high heat until it just begins to boil. Reduce heat to low, cover and simmer for 10 minutes. Use a small strainer or slotted spoon to remove the star anise, whole cloves and ginger pieces from the broth.

Carefully add halibut, skin side down, and green onions to the pot. Once soup begins to simmer again, cover pan and cook for 3 to 5 minutes, until halibut is just cooked through. Turn off heat and let rest, covered, for about 5 minutes.

For each serving, place about 1/2 cup cooked noodles in the bottom of a soup bowl. Top noodles with a piece of halibut, then pour on 1 cup of broth. Serve with condiments for diners to add as desired: bean sprouts, basil, jalapeno, lime wedges and chili oil.

Serves 4

Soups & Stews

Mediterranean Halibut Soup

    3 tablespoons olive oil
    1 1/2 pounds red-skinned potatoes, peeled and cut into 1" cubes
    1 teaspoon paprika
    1 teaspoon cumin
    1 large pinch dried red pepper flakes (more or less to taste)
    3 cups low-sodium chicken broth
    1 can (14 ounces) diced tomatoes
    1 tablespoon fresh mint, finely chopped (or 1 teaspoon dried mint)
    2 tablespoons lemon juice
    Salt and pepper to taste
    1 pound skinless halibut fillet, cut into 1" cubes
    1/4 cup fresh parsley, finely chopped

Heat oil over medium heat in a dutch oven or soup pot. Add potatoes, paprika, cumin and red pepper flakes. Stir to coat potatoes with spices then reduce heat to low, cover and cook, stirring occasionally, until potatoes begin to cook, about 5 minutes.

Add chicken broth, tomatoes, mint and lemon juice and stir to mix well. Continue cooking on low heat, covered, until potatoes are cooked through, about 10 minutes. Season broth to taste with salt and pepper then stir in halibut cubes and parsley. Turn heat off, cover pot and let fish cook in hot soup for about 10 minutes or until cooked through.

Serves 4

Halibut, Couscous and Zucchini Stew

    2 tablespoons olive oil
    1/2 cup diced onion
    1 medium zucchini, cut into quarters then into 1" pieces
    3 garlic cloves, minced or pressed
    1 tablespoon ground cumin
    1/2 teaspoon ground cinnamon
    1/2 teaspoon paprika
    1/4 teaspoon ground ginger
    Pinch of saffron
    1 teaspoon salt
    1/2 teaspoon pepper
    4 cups chicken broth
    1/2 cup raisins
    1 can (15 ounces) chickpeas, drained
    1 1/2 cups pearl (Israeli) couscous (see **Note**)
    2 medium tomatoes, cut into 1" chunks
    1 pound cooked halibut (skin and bones removed), broken into bite-sized pieces
    2 tablespoons chopped fresh mint
    2 tablespoons chopped parsley

Heat olive oil over medium heat in a large saucepan or small Dutch oven. Add onion, zucchini and garlic and cook, stirring frequently, until onion begins to soften and brown, about 5 minutes. Add cumin, cinnamon, paprika, ginger, saffron, salt and pepper; stir briefly to combine, then stir in chicken broth. Cover pot, reduce heat and allow broth to simmer for about 10 minutes. Stir in raisins, chickpeas and couscous; cover and cook another 5 minutes, then turn off heat and let stand, covered, for about 10 minutes.

Turn heat to medium and add tomatoes and halibut. Stir gently and cook until halibut is heated through, about 2 to 3 minutes. Stir in mint and parsley and serve.

Note: Pearl or Israeli couscous is a large, pearl-shaped version of traditional couscous. If you can't find it you can substitute a small pasta such as *acine de pepe* or orzo.

Serves 4

Halibut, Squash and Ginger Soup

1 tablespoon butter
1 tablespoon olive oil
1 large mild onion, chopped
1 clove garlic, pressed or minced
1 tablespoon ginger, peeled and grated finely
1 teaspoon ground cumin
1 teaspoon chili powder
2 pounds winter squash (such as pumpkin, or butternut or Hubbard squash), peeled, seeded and cut into 1/2" to 3/4" cubes
1 teaspoon fresh thyme leaves
6 cups chicken or vegetable broth
1 pound halibut (skin and bones removed), cut into 1" cubes
Salt and freshly ground black pepper

Heat the butter and olive oil over medium-high heat in a Dutch oven. Add the onion, garlic, ginger, cumin and chili powder. Reduce heat to medium low and cook, stirring occasionally, until the onion is soft but not brown, about 10 minutes.

Add the squash, thyme and broth. Bring to a boil, reduce heat, cover and simmer until squash is just done, 15 to 20 minutes. Remove about half the squash chunks to a blender or food processor. Carefully purée, adding a little broth from the pot if needed, until smooth. Return the purée to the pot and stir to mix well.

Reheat soup over medium heat. Stir in the halibut chunks, cover and cook until fish is done, about 4 to 5 minutes. Season with salt and pepper to taste and serve.

Serves 4

Main Courses

Basic Oven-Roasted Halibut

This is probably the quickest and easiest way to cook halibut. You can season the fish with any herbs or spices you want, but just a simple sprinkling of salt and pepper is all you really need.

>3/4 pound to 1 pound halibut fillet (with skin on)
>Extra virgin olive oil
>Salt and pepper

Preheat oven to 500°.

Cut fillet into 2 serving sized pieces. Line a rimmed baking sheet with aluminum foil. Brush foil with olive oil; arrange halibut pieces in pan, skin-side down. Brush fish with additional olive oil and season with salt and pepper to taste.

Place pan in oven and immediately reduce heat to 450°. Bake without turning for 8 to 10 minutes, depending on thickness, until fish is just opaque in the center.

Serves 2

Basic Poached Halibut

    2 tablespoons lemon juice
    3 or 4 slices of lemon
    1 pound halibut fillet

Fill a deep, straight-sided skillet half full of water. Add lemon juice and lemon slices and bring to a boil.

Reduce heat to low and carefully add halibut. If necessary, add more water so it just covers the fish. Cover the pan and simmer 6 to 10 minutes, depending on the thickness of fillet. Test for doneness by cutting into center; fish is done when it is just opaque. When done, carefully remove with a spatula and let cool.

Makes about 2 to 3 cup of chopped or flaked fish.

Basic Steamed Halibut

    3 or 4 slices of lemon
    1 tablespoon lemon juice
    1 pound skinless halibut fillet, cut to fit into steamer

Fit a steamer rack (sprayed with non-stick cooking spray) into a deep, straight-sided skillet or saucepan (or use a bamboo steamer lined with a piece of parchment to keep fish from sticking to steamer). Place about 1" of water in bottom of pan (water should not touch the steamer). Add lemon slices to the water and bring to a boil.

Reduce heat to low. Sprinkle fish with lemon juice, arrange it in the steamer, cover pan and simmer 6 to 10 minutes, depending on thickness of fillet. Halibut is done when it is just opaque in the center. When done, carefully remove fish with a spatula and let cool.

Makes about 2 to 3 cups of chopped or flaked fish.

Main Courses

Baked Halibut with Bread Crumb Topping

3 tablespoons dry bread crumbs
3 tablespoons olive oil, divided
1 tablespoon finely chopped flatleaf parsley
1/4 teaspoon salt, divided
2 tablespoons fresh lemon juice
1 large clove of garlic, minced or pressed
3/4 pound to 1 pound skinless halibut fillet, about 1" thick

Preheat oven to 400°F.

Combine bread crumbs, 1 tablespoon olive oil, parsley and 1/8 teaspoon salt in a small bowl and set aside.

In a shallow bowl or pie plate, whisk together remaining 2 tablespoons of olive oil with the lemon juice, 1/8 teaspoon salt and garlic. Pat fish dry with a paper towel then place it in the olive oil and lemon juice mixture, turning to coat all sides. Let fish stand for about 5 minutes, turning once, then transfer fish to a baking pan. Sprinkle crumbs in an even, loose layer over the top of the fish (do not press down on crumbs). Bake uncovered for 18 to 22 minutes or until fish is cooked through and crumb topping is golden brown.

Serves 2

Baked Halibut Fillets

Thanks for this quick and easy recipe go to my friend and recipe tester, Susan Sullivan.

   1 pound halibut fillet
   1 tablespoon lemon juice
   1/8 teaspoon paprika
   Dash of salt and pepper
   1 tablespoon butter
   1 tablespoon flour
   1/2 cup milk
   1/4 cup bread crumbs
   1 tablespoon minced parsley

Preheat oven to 350°.

Cut fillet into serving size pieces, and place in a greased, shallow baking dish. Sprinkle with lemon juice, paprika, salt and pepper.

In a saucepan, melt butter and blend in flour. Slowly add milk and cook, stirring constantly, until thick and bubbly. Season to taste with salt and pepper. Pour sauce over fillets then sprinkle with bread crumbs. Bake for 25 to 35 minutes, depending on thickness of fillet. Sprinkle with parsley and serve.

Serves 2 to 3

Recipes From Alaska's Best Chefs

Paradiso's Baked Halibut

Chef George Pitsilionos
Paradiso's Restaurant, Kenai

1/2 cup olive oil
1/2 cup white wine
1/4 cup water
3 large ripe tomatoes, thinly sliced
8 large cloves of garlic, thinly sliced
2 pounds halibut fillet (1" to 1 1/2" thick)
Salt and pepper
2 tablespoons coarsely chopped Italian (flat-leaf) parsley
Lemon wedges (for garnish)

Preheat oven to 425°.

Cover bottom of a medium-sized baking pan with olive oil, wine and water. Add a layer of half the sliced tomatoes topped with half the sliced garlic. Place the halibut on the tomatoes and garlic; season with salt and pepper and sprinkle with chopped parsley. Top the parsley with another layer of tomatoes and garlic.

Cover pan with aluminum foil and bake 20 minutes. Uncover and continue baking for another 10 to 15 minutes, or until fish is done and tomatoes begin to brown. Garnish with lemon wedges.

Serves 4 to 6

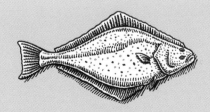

Baked Halibut with Vermouth

This was one of my mother's favorite ways to cook halibut.

    3/4 pound to 1 pound halibut steaks or fillets
    2 tablespoons dry vermouth or dry white wine
    1/2 teaspoon dried thyme
    3 tablespoons butter
    1 large shallot, minced
    Juice of 1 lemon
    2 tablespoons capers, rinsed and drained

Preheat oven to 375°.

Place halibut in a small, greased baking pan. Drizzle with vermouth and sprinkle with thyme. Cover pan tightly with foil and bake 20 to 25 minutes, depending on thickness of fish.

While halibut cooks, melt butter in a small skillet over medium heat and sauté shallots until soft but not brown. Stir in lemon juice and capers. Turn off heat and let sauce stand until halibut is done.

To serve, divide halibut into two portions. Place fish on plates and spoon sauce over the top.

Serves 2

Main Courses

Halibut à L'Orange

1 tablespoon butter
3 tablespoons vegetable oil, divided
1/2 cup onion, finely diced
1/2 cup flour, divided
1/4 cup chicken broth
1/2 cup fresh-squeezed orange juice (from 2 oranges)
1/4 teaspoon salt
Dash of pepper
1 teaspoon orange zest
1 1/2 pounds skinless halibut fillet
2 tablespoons parsley, finely chopped

Melt the butter and 1 tablespoon of the vegetable oil in a non-stick skillet over medium heat. Add the onion and cook, stirring often, until translucent, about 3 minutes. Stir in 1 tablespoon of the flour, the chicken broth, orange juice, salt and pepper. Cook, stirring often, until sauce thickens and is smooth, about 10 minutes. Stir in the orange zest; reduce heat to low and keep sauce warm while preparing the halibut fillets.

Cut the halibut into 4 equal pieces; dust the fish with the remaining flour. Heat the remaining vegetable oil in a non-stick skillet over medium-high heat. Add the halibut and cook until golden brown and done, turning once (about 6 to 8 minutes, depending on thickness).

Transfer fillets to a warm serving platter. Stir the sauce then spoon over the fish, sprinkle with parsley and serve.

Serves 4

Halibut Amandine

    2 tablespoons vegetable oil, divided
    3 tablespoons butter, divided
    Salt and pepper
    1 1/2 to 2 pounds skinless halibut fillets, cut into 4 portions
    1/4 cup sliced almonds
    2 tablespoons fresh-squeezed lemon juice
    2 tablespoons dry white wine
    2 tablespoons chopped parsley

Melt 1 tablespoon butter with 1 tablespoon oil in a heavy skillet over medium high heat until butter foams but does not brown. Season halibut with salt and pepper and add to pan. Reduce heat to medium and cook fish, turning once, until it is just done in the center, about 8 to 10 minutes. Remove fish to a warm platter.

Increase heat in skillet to medium high; add remaining 2 tablespoons butter and 1 tablespoon oil. When butter is melted, add almonds and cook, stirring constantly, just until they turn light brown. Turn off heat and stir in lemon juice and white wine.

Pour almond mixture over the halibut fillets, sprinkle with parsley and serve.

Serves 4

Main Courses

Halibut Caddy Ganty

This recipe was shared by Dave and JoAnn Lesh, owners of Alaska's Gustavus Inn. The recipe was originally collected by the Inn's founder, Sully Lesh, who explained its source: "A neighbor brought it in to me one day written exactly as her husband had written it, as it was told to him by a fisherman from Pelican, Alaska, who got it from Caddy Ganty herself." Caddy was the wife of Pros Ganty, one of the founders of Pelican Cold Storage in the 1920s. This is the Gustavus Inn's most frequently requested recipe.

> 2 pounds halibut fillets, fresh or defrosted
> White wine to cover
> Sourdough bread crumbs
> 2 cups sour cream
> 1 cup mayonnaise, bottled or homemade (recipe on page 88)
> 1 cup finely chopped onions
> Paprika

Cut the halibut into pieces approximately 3" by 3" and 1" thick and put into a bowl, lightly salting and pouring wine over each layer until the pieces are all in and the wine covers all the fish. Cover the bowl and set it in a cool place to marinate for 2 hours.

Preheat oven to 350°. Drain the fillets and pat dry with paper towels or cloth, then roll in dry bread crumbs (the Inn uses dried homemade sourdough bread and grinds the crumbs in the grater of their mixer). Place the crumbed fillets in a single layer in a lightly buttered baking dish which can be brought to the table.

Mix sour cream, mayonnaise and chopped onions and spread thickly on top of the fillets, smoothing it out to the edges so the fish is covered completely. Sprinkle the top with paprika and bake for 20 to 30 minutes or until light brown and bubbly and an instant read thermometer registers 125° in the thickest part. Serve at once.

Serves 4

Halibut Poached in Cream

This is a great way to revive halibut that has dried out from being in the freezer just a bit too long.

- 1 to 1 1/2 pounds skinless halibut fillet, at least 1" thick
- Salt and pepper
- 1 tablespoon butter
- 1 cup half-and-half (or more if needed)
- 1/4 cup sour cream (not fat free)
- 1/4 cup sun-dried tomatoes, drained and chopped
- 4 to 6 large basil leaves, sliced into thin ribbons

Cut halibut into 4 equal-sized serving pieces and season with salt and pepper. Choose a saucepan or deep skillet (preferably non-stick) that is just large enough to accommodate the pieces of fish in a single layer without crowding. Melt butter in pan over medium-high heat. Reduce heat to medium-low and place fish in pan; pour in enough half-and-half so that it comes at least halfway up the sides of the halibut pieces.

Cover pan and allow cream to come just to a simmer (small bubbles will form around the edges). Do not let it boil hard. Once cream is simmering, reduce heat again to low and allow halibut to poach for 6 to 8 minutes (spoon cream over the top of the fish several times while it cooks) or until it is opaque in the center. Carefully remove fish pieces to a serving plate and keep warm.

Return skillet to medium heat and and let cream boil gently, uncovered, until it thickens slightly and reduces by about half, stirring often to prevent scorching. Remove pan from heat and add the sour cream, stirring until smooth, then stir in the tomatoes and basil. Pour sauce over halibut and serve.

Serves 4

Main Courses

Halibut with Creamy Mushroom Sauce

    2 tablespoons butter
    2 cups (about 1/4 pound) assorted fresh mushrooms, sliced
    1 large shallot, finely diced
    1 cup sour cream (not fat free)
    1/4 cup sherry, white wine or chicken broth
    1 1/2 to 2 pounds halibut fillets, cut into 4 equal portions
    1 teaspoon of salt
    1/2 teaspoon pepper
    2 tablespoons chopped parsley, for garnish

Preheat oven to 425°.

Melt butter over medium heat in a large skillet. Add mushrooms and shallots and cook, stirring often, until both are soft and golden brown, about 10 minutes. Turn off heat; stir in sour cream and sherry and mix until smooth. (Do not let sauce boil after adding sour cream.) Cover and keep sauce warm while halibut cooks.

Season halibut with salt and pepper and place in a greased, shallow baking dish. Bake for 10 to 15 minutes, depending on thickness, until fish flakes with a fork.

Pour sauce over halibut, sprinkle with parsley and serve.

Serves 4

Glacier Brewhouse Halibut with Raspberry-Roasted Shallot Butter

Chef Patrick Hoogerhyde
Glacier Brewhouse, Anchorage

3/4 pound halibut fillet, cut into 2 portions
2 teaspoons olive oil
1/2 teaspoon sea salt
2 tablespoons Raspberry-Roasted Shallot Butter (recipe below)
1 1/2 cups prepared creamy polenta (for serving)
2 cups Spinach and Herbs (recipe on facing page)
2 tablespoons Blackberry Vinaigrette (recipe on facing page)
8 to 12 fresh raspberries (for garnish)
1 teaspoon gremolata (for garnish)

Rub fish with oil, season with sea salt and grill to medium rare or desired doneness. Divide polenta between 2 plates. Top with fish then Raspberry-Roasted Shallot Butter. Toss Spinach and Herbs with Blackberry Vinaigrette and place alongside the halibut. Garnish with fresh berries and gremolata.

Serves 2

Raspberry-Roasted Shallot Butter

1/4 pound butter, softened
2 teaspoons parsley, chopped
1/2 a medium shallot, roasted and minced
1 tablespoon raspberry purée
1/4 cup frozen raspberries, thawed and chopped
2 teaspoons roasted garlic, minced
1 tablespoon fresh basil, coarsely chopped

Whip softened butter in mixer with wire whip on low speed for approximately 5 minutes. Butter will turn slightly white. Fold in all remaining ingredients and blend thoroughly. Label and date. Store in refrigerator until needed. Makes about 1 cup.

Spinach and Herbs

2 cups spinach, stems removed
1/4 cup Italian parsley, leaves only

Mix and serve.

Serves 2

Blackberry Vinaigrette

1/4 cup canola oil
1/4 cup olive oil
1/4 cup red wine vinegar
1 tablespoon honey
4 ounces frozen blackberries or marionberries, chopped in food processor
1 teaspoon Dijon mustard
1 tablespoon chopped shallots
1 clove garlic, chopped
2 teaspoons fresh thyme, chopped
2 teaspoons fresh parsley, chopped
2 teaspoons fresh oregano, chopped
1/4 teaspoon Kosher salt
1/8 teaspoon fresh-cracked black pepper

Combine all ingredients and whisk together to mix well. Taste and adjust seasonings if needed. Store in refrigerator. Shake well before using. Makes about 1 cup.

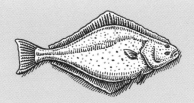

Halibut Gratin

    1 tablespoon vegetable oil
    1 small shallot, finely chopped
    4 medium white mushroom caps, cut in half and thinly sliced
    3/4 pound halibut fillet, cut into 3/4" to 1" cubes
    1/2 cup heavy cream
    1/4 teaspoon salt
    Dash of black pepper
    1 tablespoon sherry (optional)
    3 tablespoons Panko (Japanese-style bread crumbs)
    1 tablespoon grated Parmesan cheese
    1 tablespoon butter, melted

Preheat broiler to high.

In a non-stick skillet, heat oil over medium-high heat. Add shallots and mushrooms and cook, stirring often, until shallots soften and mushrooms begin to brown, about 5 minutes. Lower heat to medium-low and stir in fish cubes, cream, salt and pepper. Cover and cook, stirring gently once or twice, until fish is just done, about 3 to 4 minutes. Remove pan from heat and stir in sherry, if using.

Divide mixture between 2 small gratin dishes, clean scallop shells, or other shallow, individual oven-proof dishes. In a small bowl, combine Panko and Parmesan cheese and sprinkle evenly over halibut mixture. Drizzle melted butter over the top. Place dishes on a baking sheet and place under broiler, watching constantly, until topping begins to brown (about 1 minute).

Serves 2

Halibut Olympia

There are many different Halibut Olympia recipes, all variations on Halibut Caddy Ganty. This is my favorite version.

> 4 tablespoons butter, divided
> 1 tablespoon vegetable oil
> 2 medium yellow onions, thinly sliced
> 1 teaspoon sugar
> Salt and pepper
> 1 1/2 to 2 pounds skinless halibut fillet, cut into 4 serving pieces
> 1/2 cup mayonnaise, bottled or homemade (recipe on page 88)
> 1/2 cup sour cream (not fat free)
> 1 clove garlic, minced or pressed
> 3/4 cup Panko (Japanese-style bread crumbs) or other dry bread crumbs

Preheat oven to 400°.

Melt 1 tablespoon butter with the vegetable oil in a large, non-stick skillet over medium-high heat. Add onions and sprinkle with sugar and salt and pepper to taste. Cook, stirring often, until onions are soft and well-browned.

Rub a medium sized baking dish with 1 tablespoon butter; arrange halibut pieces in a single layer and season with salt and pepper. Mix mayonnaise, sour cream and garlic in a small bowl then spread evenly over fish. Spoon the browned onions over the mayonnaise-sour cream layer. Melt remaining 2 tablespoons butter in the skillet and stir in bread crumbs. Sprinkle buttered crumbs over the top of the onions.

Bake fish for 20 to 25 minutes, until fish is done and crumb topping is golden brown. Serve immediately.

Serves 4

Halibut Pot Pie

    1 tablespoon vegetable oil
    1 cup roughly chopped onions
    1 cup sliced mushrooms
    1 large potato, peeled and cut into 1/2" cubes
    3 tablespoons butter
    3 tablespoons flour
    1/2 teaspoon salt
    1/4 teaspoon black pepper
    1/2 teaspoon seafood seasoning (such as Old Bay®)
    2 cups whole milk
    2 cups cooked halibut (about 1 pound), broken into large pieces
    1/2 cup peas, fresh or frozen
    1 sheet frozen puff pastry, thawed

Preheat oven to 350°.

Heat vegetable oil over medium-high heat in a large skillet. Add onions, mushrooms and potato cubes. Cook, stirring often, until onions begin to brown, 4 or 5 minutes. Reduce heat to medium-low, cover pan and continue to cook until potatoes are almost done, about 5 minutes more, stirring often. Spoon vegetables into a bowl and set aside.

Wipe out skillet with paper towels. Over medium heat, melt butter then stir in flour, mixing until smooth. Add salt, pepper and seafood seasoning and cook, stirring constantly, for about 2 minutes. Slowly whisk in milk and cook, stirring often, until sauce thickens and begins to bubble around the edges.

Remove pan from heat and stir in cooked vegetables, halibut pieces and peas. Pour mixture into medium-sized, greased casserole, deep-dish pie plate or quiche pan. Cut puff pastry sheet to fit top and place over the halibut mixture. Cut several vents in crust for steam to escape. Bake pot pie for 20 to 30 minutes, until filling is bubbly and crust is golden brown.

Serves 4 to 6

Main Courses

Stuffed Halibut Fillets

    3 slices bacon, finely chopped
    3 ounces cream cheese (not fat-free), at room temperature
    2 tablespoons minced chives
    1 pinch cayenne pepper OR several drops of Tabasco® sauce (to taste)
    1 1/2 to 2 pounds skinless halibut fillet, at least 1" thick
    1/2 cup dry bread crumbs
    1 tablespoon finely minced parsley (or 1 teaspoon dry parsley)
    1/2 teaspoon salt
    1/8 teaspoon black pepper
    1 tablespoon vegetable oil

Cook chopped bacon in a small skillet until crisp. Remove and drain on paper towels. In a small bowl, combine bacon with cream cheese, chives and pepper flakes (or Tabasco®). Refrigerate at least 30 minutes before proceeding.

Preheat oven to 375°.

Cut halibut fillets into 4 serving pieces. Cut a deep pocket into the side of each piece, being careful not to cut all the way through. Place a heaping spoonful of filling into each pocket. Firmly press the edge of the pocket closed (if necessary, secure with a toothpick). Mix bread crumbs, parsley, salt and pepper and spread on a plate. Press both sides of stuffed fillets into crumbs, coating evenly.

Heat oil in an oven-safe skillet over medium-high heat. Add fillets and cook until golden brown, about 2 minutes. Turn fillets; place skillet in the oven and continue cooking until halibut is just cooked through, about 5 to 7 minutes.

Serves 4

Halibut and Shiitake Packets

> 2 tablespoons peanut or other vegetable oil
> 2 teaspoons sesame oil
> 1 tablespoon rice vinegar
> 2 tablespoons bottled oyster sauce
> 1 medium garlic clove, minced or pressed
> 1 teaspoon freshly grated ginger (optional)
> 1 cup (about 4 ounces) thinly sliced shiitake mushroom caps (remove and discard stems)
> 1 large mild, sweet onion (such as Vidalia), thinly sliced
> 4 teaspoons Chinese rice wine, dry sherry or dry white wine
> 1 1/2 to 2 pounds halibut fillets, about 1" thick
> Salt and pepper
> Chopped flat-leaf parsley

Preheat oven to 450°F.

In a small bowl, whisk together peanut oil, sesame oil, rice vinegar, oyster sauce, garlic and ginger until combined. Spoon about half of the sauce over the mushroom slices and toss to coat. Set aside.

Cut 4 large pieces of heavy duty foil (about 12" square) and place them diagonally on the counter (with one corner of the square at the bottom). Separate onion slices into rings and place 1/4 of them just below the center of each piece of foil. Sprinkle about 1 teaspoon of wine over each pile of onions.

Cut halibut into 4 equal portions and pat dry with paper towels. Season with salt and pepper and place on top of onions. Spoon the mushrooms on top of the fish, dividing them equally, then drizzle remaining sauce equally over the mushrooms. Fold the back corner of the foil toward you over the fish to form a triangular packet. Double-fold and crimp all edges, sealing the packets tightly.

Place the sealed packets on a large, rimmed baking sheet and bake for 15 minutes. Remove from oven and promptly slit packets open to allow steam to escape and prevent overcooking. Place opened packets on plates or remove the contents to plates before serving (spoon juices from the packet over the fish); sprinkle with parsley.

Serves 4

Main Courses

Asian Halibut Stir-Fry

    1/4 cup low-sodium soy sauce
    2 teaspoons sesame oil
    1 tablespoon sugar
    2 teaspoons finely grated ginger
    1 large clove of garlic, minced or pressed
    1 large scallion, finely chopped
    2 tablespoons vegetable oil, divided
    1/2 to 3/4 pound halibut fillet, cut into 1" chunks
    1/2 cup sliced carrots
    1/2 medium green or red bell pepper, cut into strips
    1/2 medium onion, cut into 1/4" slices
    2 teaspoons cornstarch dissolved in 2 tablespoons water
    2 cups cooked rice

In a small bowl, combine soy sauce, sesame oil, sugar, ginger, garlic and scallion. Set aside and let sauce mixture stand at room temperature for at least 20 minutes to develop flavors.

Heat 1 tablespoon oil in a large, nonstick skillet or wok over medium high heat. Add the halibut chunks and cook, gently stirring often, until fish is almost done (about 3 to 4 minutes). Carefully remove fish to a dish and set aside.

In same skillet, heat remaining tablespoon of oil (if needed) over medium-high heat and add carrots, green pepper and onion. Cook and stir until vegetables soften, about 5 minutes. Return halibut to pan with vegetables.

Stir the cornstarch and water mixture into the sauce mixture and add to skillet. Cook, stirring gently to avoid breaking up the fish, until sauce thickens and begins to boil and fish and vegetables are coated with sauce. Remove pan from heat; serve fish and vegetables with rice.

Makes 2 servings

Stir-Fried Halibut with Mushrooms and Asparagus

 3/4 cup low-sodium chicken broth
 2 tablespoons oyster sauce
 2 tablespoons rice wine or sherry (optional)
 1 teaspoon sugar
 1 teaspoon finely grated fresh ginger
 1 large clove of garlic, minced or pressed
 2 teaspoons corn starch
 4 teaspoons vegetable oil, divided
 2 large portobello mushrooms (about 6 ounces), stems removed, caps halved and sliced about 1/2" thick
 3 scallions, white and green parts, halved lengthwise and cut into 1" pieces
 6 to 8 stalks of asparagus, ends trimmed, cut into 1" pieces
 3/4 pound halibut fillet cut into 1" cubes
 2 cups cooked rice

Combine chicken broth, oyster sauce, rice wine or sherry, sugar, ginger and garlic in a small bowl. Spoon about 2 tablespoons of this mixture over the halibut chunks, mix to coat well and set aside. Add the corn starch to the remaining sauce ingredients, stir well and set aside.

Heat 2 teaspoons of vegetable oil in a large non-stick skillet over medium-high heat. Add mushrooms and cook, stirring often, for about 4 to 5 minutes. Add green onions and asparagus and continue cooking and stirring until mushrooms are beginning to brown and asparagus is bright green, another 2 to 3 minutes. Remove vegetables to a bowl.

Add remaining 2 teaspoons of oil to the skillet. Add the halibut; stir gently and cook until fish begins turning opaque, about 3 minutes. Return mushrooms and asparagus to pan. Stir sauce mixture and add to fish and vegetables. Cook and stir gently until sauce thickens and fish is cooked through. Serve with cooked rice.

Serves 2

Homestead Halibut with Sweet Pea and Lemon Risotto

Chef Chris Lukic
The Homestead Restaurant, Homer

- 3 cups arborio rice
- 9 cups water or chicken stock
- 2 cups frozen peas or fresh
- 1/2 cup canola oil
- 1 cup all purpose flour
- 6 to 8 pieces of halibut fillet, about 8 ounces each
- 2 lemons, peeled, segments removed and chopped
- 1 1/2 tablespoons butter
- 1 cup Parmesan cheese
- Olive oil and lemon juice (for garnish)

Prepare risotto: Place rice in a large saucepan. Turn on medium heat and stir until rice is lightly toasted. Slowly pour in 1 cup water or stock and stir until stock is absorbed. Add another 1 cup water or stock and stir slowly until gone. Continue adding the water or stock 1 cup at a time until you have used all but 1 cup. This should take about 14 minutes. Remove the risotto from the heat and let sit.

Place the peas in a blender and purée until the mixture is the consistency of mashed potatoes (if necessary, add room temperature water). Set aside.

Preheat oven to 350°. Heat canola oil in a large sauté pan over medium heat. Lightly dredge halibut fillets in flour and place in pan. When the halibut is lightly golden on the bottom flip over and place in oven for 4 to 5 minutes. Remove from oven and keep warm.

While halibut is in the oven return the risotto to the stove over medium heat. Add the remaining 1 cup water or stock and simmer until gone. Add the pea purée and lemon segments and simmer for about 1 minute. Stir in butter and cheese until melted. Add salt and pepper to taste. To serve, place 1 cup risotto on plate or in a bowl and place 1 piece of halibut on top. Drizzle olive oil and fresh lemon juice on top and serve.

Serves 6 to 8

Korean Halibut with Bok Choy and Eggplant

    3 tablespoons vegetable oil, divided
    3 cloves garlic, minced or pressed
    1/2 teaspoon red pepper flakes (more or less to taste)
    1/2 cup low-sodium soy sauce
    2 tablespoons bottled oyster sauce
    3 tablespoons (packed) brown sugar
    2 teaspoons finely grated fresh ginger
    1 tablespoon sesame oil
    2 medium Japanese eggplants, ends trimmed
    4 baby bok choy
    Salt and pepper
    1 to 1 1/2 pounds halibut fillet, about 1" thick, cut into 4 pieces
    2 scallions, thinly sliced on the diagonal

Heat 1 tablespoon vegetable oil in a small saucepan over medium heat. Add garlic and red pepper flakes; cook, stirring constantly, for 1 minute, being careful not to burn garlic. Stir in soy sauce, oyster sauce, brown sugar, ginger, sesame oil and 1/2 cup water. Raise heat to high and bring to a boil; reduce heat to low and simmer for 5 to 10 minutes. Remove from heat and set sauce aside.

Preheat broiler to high; arrange oven rack so top of food will be about 6" from the heat. Line a broiler pan or large sheet pan with rack with foil; spray foil and rack with non-stick cooking spray.

Cut eggplants and bok choy in half lengthwise and place them in a large bowl. Pour on 1 tablespoon vegetable oil and toss to coat well. Season vegetables with salt and pepper. Brush both sides of fish with remaining 1 tablespoon vegetable oil; season with salt and pepper. Arange fish and vegetables on prepared broiler pan.

Stir sauce and remove 1/2 cup to a small bowl for serving. Brush fish and vegetables with some of the remaining sauce and place in the broiler. Cook until vegetables are tender and golden brown and fish is just done, turning all occasionally and brushing with remaining sauce. (If necessary, remove fish first and continue cooking vegetables until they are done.) Arrange fish and vegetables on a platter and sprinkle with sliced scallions. Pass the reserved sauce at the table.

Serves 4

Main Courses

Pan-Seared Halibut with Sesame-Ginger Vinaigrette

    2 tablespoons vegetable oil
    1 tablespoon sesame oil
    1 tablespoon rice vinegar
    1 teaspoon sugar
    2 teaspoons finely grated fresh ginger (or 1/2 teaspoon dry ginger)
    1 clove garlic, minced or pressed
    2 tablespoons sesame seeds
    1 tablespoon all-purpose flour
    1/4 teaspoon salt
    1/8 teaspoon black pepper
    3/4 pound to 1 pound halibut fillet, skin on
    1 tablespoon butter or vegetable oil

Preheat oven to 400°.

Prepare Sesame Ginger-Vinaigrette: In a small bowl, whisk together vegetable oil, sesame oil, rice vinegar, sugar, ginger and garlic until well combined. Set aside.

On a large plate or pie pan, mix sesame seeds, flour, salt and pepper.

Brush 1 tablespoon of vinaigrette over the top of the halibut. Press the halibut into the sesame seed mixture, coating the top completely (do not coat the skin side).

Melt butter over medium heat in an oven-proof skillet. When pan is hot, add halibut, sesame-seed side down, and cook for 2 to 3 minutes, or until golden brown (do not let sesame seeds burn). Using a spatula and being careful not to disturb the sesame coating, turn the fillet over onto the skin side. Place skillet in oven and continue cooking for 6 to 10 minutes (depending on thickness), or until halibut is opaque in the middle and the fish flakes easily with a fork.

Place halibut on a serving dish and drizzle with remaining Sesame-Ginger Vinaigrette.

Serves 2

Homer Wahoo Halibut Tacos

This recipe, created by Teri Robl, was originally printed in the Homer News. Teri has kindly given me permission to include the recipe in this book.

    1 pound halibut fillets
    2 tablespoons butter, melted
    1/2 teaspoon lemon pepper seasoning
    1/8 teaspoon garlic powder
    1/2 teaspoon ground cumin
    8 corn or flour tortillas, 6" diameter
    1 cup coleslaw mix or shredded cabbage or lettuce
    Creamy Avocado Sauce (recipe on opposite page)

Preheat oven to 450°. Prepare Creamy Avocado Sauce; add about 1/4 cup to the coleslaw mix in a medium bowl and toss well. Set aside while you prepare the halibut.

Cut halibut fillet crosswise into 3/4" slices. Place fish in a single layer in a shallow, greased baking pan. Combine melted butter, lemon pepper, garlic powder and cumin in a small bowl. Brush mixture over fish. Bake halibut for 4 to 6 minutes or until fish flakes easily with a fork.

Warm tortillas by wrapping in foil and heating in the oven while the fish bakes, or wrap them in a towel and microwave on high for 30 seconds.

To assemble: Spoon some of the coleslaw mixture onto each tortilla, add fish slices then fold tortilla over filling. Suggested additions are mango or papaya salsa, picante sauce or hot sauce.

Serves 4

Main Courses

Creamy Avocado Sauce

    1 ripe avocado, peeled and chopped
    2 green onions, chopped
    1 to 2 cloves garlic, chopped
    1 cup sour cream
    1 cup plain yogurt
    1 cup mayonnaise, bottled or homemade (recipe on page 88)
    2 teaspoons green Tabasco® sauce
    1 teaspoon apple cider vinegar
    1 teaspoon lime juice
    1 teaspoon lemon pepper seasoning
    1/4 teaspoon salt

Place all ingredients in a food processor and process until smooth. Adjust amounts of seasonings according to your own tastes.

Makes about 4 cups

THE FISHERMAN'S WIFE

Halibut Cheeks with Bacon and Shallot Relish

Halibut cheeks are a delicacy well known in Alaska and the Pacific Northwest but perhaps unfamiliar to cooks elsewhere. The cheeks are cut from the area behind the halibut's eyes and jaw and have a flavor and texture compared to sea scallops or lobster. Just as the size of the fish from which they are cut varies, halibut cheeks also differ greatly in size, from delicate morsels that would just fit into your palm to giants larger than your entire hand. If you're lucky enough to find halibut cheeks in your market, don't pass them up.

    2 strips bacon, cut crosswise into slivers about 1/4" wide
    2 tablespoons butter
    1 medium shallot, finely diced
    1 tablespoon rice vinegar
    1/4 teaspoon sugar
    1 tablespoon chopped flat-leaf parsley
    1 tablespoon olive oil
    3/4 pound to 1 pound halibut cheeks
    Salt and pepper

Heat a small non stick skillet over medium-high heat. Add the bacon slivers and cook, stirring often, until bacon is browned and crisp. Using a slotted spoon, remove bacon pieces to paper towels to drain; if necessary, pour off all but about 1 tablespoon of bacon fat. Reduce heat to medium and add butter to bacon fat in skillet. When butter has melted, add shallots and cook, stirring often, until they turn light brown and begin to caramelize, 4 to 5 minutes. Add bacon pieces back to pan; stir and continue cooking another 1 to 2 minutes. Stir in vinegar, sugar and parsley then remove relish from heat and keep warm.

Heat olive oil in a large non-stick skillet over medium high heat. Season halibut cheeks with salt and pepper then add to pan. Cook 2 to 3 minutes then turn and cook an additional 2 to 3 minutes, until cheeks are almost firm to the touch. Do not overcook. Place halibut cheeks on plates, spoon relish over fish and serve immediately.

Serves 2

Crab-Stuffed Halibut Cheeks

   1/2 cup crab meat (fresh, canned or frozen), drained
   1/4 cup (about 2 ounces) cream cheese, softened (not fat free)
   1 tablespoon mayonnaise, bottled or homemade (recipe on page 88)
   2 green onions, finely chopped
   Pinch of cayenne
   1 pound halibut cheeks
   2 tablespoons butter, melted
   Salt and pepper

In a small bowl, combine crab meat, cream cheese, mayonnaise, green onions and cayenne. Refreigerate at least 30 minutes before proceeding with recipe.

Place oven rack about 6" from heat source and preheat broiler to high.

Pat halibut cheeks dry. With a small, sharp knife, cut a pocket into the side of each cheek, being careful not to cut all the way through. Spoon a scant tablespoon of the stuffing into each pocket, then press edges firmly to close (secure with a toothpick if necessary).

Place halibut cheeks on a broiler pan or rack set over a baking sheet. Brush cheeks with melted butter; sprinkle with salt and pepper. Broil for 3 minutes then turn and continue cooking for 2 to 4 minutes, until halibut cheeks are just cooked through. Do not overcook.

Serves 2 to 3

Jens' Halibut Meunière à la Bonne Femme

Chef Jens Haagen Hansen
Jens' Restaurant, Anchorage

1 pound halibut fillet, about 1 1/2" thick
Flour
Salt and pepper
2 tablespoons olive oil

Ragout

2 tablespoons butter
1 large shallot, thinly sliced
1 large garlic clove, crushed
1 cup mixed mushrooms, thinly sliced
2 teaspoons white wine Worcestershire sauce (sold as Lea & Perrins® Marinade for Chicken)
Juice of one lemon
2 tablespoons white wine

Beurre Blanc

2 tablespoons heavy whipping cream
4 tablespoons Plugrá butter (see **Note**)
1 tablespoon chopped parsley

Cut halibut into 2 equal portions. Season with salt and pepper and dredge in flour, shaking off excess. Heat olive oil in a sauté pan over medium heat. Add halibut and cook for 3 minutes; turn fillets and cook for another 1 to 2 minutes, then remove to plates and keep warm.

Prepare the Ragout: To the sauté pan add 2 tablespoons butter, the shallot, garlic and mushrooms. Sauté for 3 minutes. Add Worcestershire, lemon juice, and white wine. Cook and reduce over medium heat until mushrooms are done, about 5 minutes.

Remove mushroom mixture with a slotted spoon and place on top of halibut; continue to keep warm.

For the Beurre Blanc, add the heavy cream to the sauté pan with the juices and let reduce for one minute. Take pan off the heat and whisk in the Plugrá butter, 1 tablespoon at a time, until all is incorporated. Add the parsley, pour sauce over halibut and serve.

Serves 2

Note: Plugrá is a European-style butter with a higher butterfat content and less moisture than regular commercial butter. It is available in specialty stores and some larger supermarkets. If you can't find it you can substitute commercial, unsalted butter, but the dish will not be as rich.

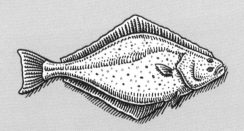

Halibut Fajitas

    3 tablespoons olive oil, divided
    1 large onion, sliced
    2 bell peppers (1 green, 1 red), cut into 1/4" strips
    2 cloves garlic, minced or pressed
    1/4 teaspoon red pepper flakes (optional, use more or less to taste)
    1 teaspoon chili powder
    1 teaspoon cumin
    1/2 teaspoon salt
    1/4 teaspoon ground black pepper
    1 1/2 to 2 pounds skinless halibut fillet, cut into 1" strips
    12 small flour tortillas, wrapped in aluminum foil and warmed in a 250° oven
    Fajita toppings (see list below)

Heat 2 tablespoons of olive oil in large skillet over high heat. Add onions, peppers garlic and red pepper flakes and cook, stirring often, until vegetables begin to soften. Remove skillet from heat, transfer vegetables to a bowl and set aside.

In a small bowl, mix chili powder, cumin, salt and black pepper. Sprinkle spice mixture over all sides of halibut strips. Heat remaining 1 tablespoon of olive oil in skillet over medium heat. Add halibut and cook, turning and stirring gently, just until fish is done (don't worry if it falls apart a bit). Add onion-pepper mixture back to skillet and continue cooking just until warmed through.

Spoon halibut and vegetables into warm tortillas and serve with desired toppings from list below.

Serves 4 to 6

Serve Halibut Fajitas with any or all of these toppings:
    Sour cream   Guacamole (or sliced avocado)
    Salsa   Shredded cheddar or Monterey Jack cheese
    Lime wedges   Coarsely chopped cilantro

Main Courses

Halibut with Mango, Red Pepper and Tomato Salsa

This delicious recipe is a creation of my friend, Davida Kapler.

    3/4 cup diced mango (see **Note**)
    1/2 cup diced red pepper
    1/2 cup diced ripe tomato
    1 tablespoon finely diced fresh jalapeno pepper
    2 tablespoons finely chopped red onion
    2 tablespoons coarsely chopped cilantro
    Juice of 1 large lime
    1 pound fresh halibut (1" to 1 1/2" thick)
    1 small clove garlic, minced or pressed
    1 teaspoon olive oil
    Salt and pepper

Preheat oven to 350°.

In a bowl, mix together mango, red pepper, tomato, jalapeno, red onion, cilantro and lime juice. Allow mixture to sit for at least 1 hour at room temperature.

Cut halibut into 2 equal pieces. Place fish in a small baking dish, rub with the garlic and sprinkle with olive oil, salt and pepper. Cover with foil and bake for 15 to 20 minutes, depending on the thickness of the fish. Remove to a warmed serving dish and top with salsa. Extra salsa can be refrigerated and used with other dishes or with chips.

Serves 2

Note: If fresh mango is not available, you can substitute about 3/4 cup frozen mango chunks, thawed, or dice up some bottled mango spears (often available in the produce section of your supermarket).

Buttermilk Fried Halibut with Spicy Slaw

This super-crispy fish, served here with coleslaw, would also be perfect for fish and chips. Be sure to make the slaw and marinate the fish at least 2 hours before you want to serve it.

- 1 1/2 to 2 pounds skinless halibut fillets, cut into 8 equal pieces
- 1 cup buttermilk, divided
- 1/4 cup mayonnaise, bottled or homemade (recipe on page 88)
- 2 tablespoons sugar
- 1/2 teaspoon prepared horseradish
- 1 tablespoon white or rice vinegar
- Salt and pepper
- 1 package (14 to 16 ounces) coleslaw mix
- 1/2 cup flour, seasoned with salt and pepper
- 1/2 cup Panko (Japanese-style bread crumbs)
- 1/2 cup peanut or other vegetable oil (for frying)

Place halibut pieces in a large zip-top plastic bag. Add 3/4 cup buttermilk and tightly seal the bag, pressing out as much air as possible. Turn the bag several times so that all of the fish is coated in buttermilk. Refrigerate at least 2 hours.

In a large bowl, whisk together the remaining 1/4 cup buttermilk, mayonnaise, sugar, horseradish, vinegar, 1/2 teaspoon salt and 1/8 teaspoon pepper until smooth. Add coleslaw mix and toss to coat well. Cover bowl and refrigerate at least 2 hours.

To prepare the fish, heat the oil in a large, deep frying pan over medium-high heat until it shimmers. Mix the seasoned flour with the Panko in a shallow dish or pie plate. Remove fish pieces from the buttermilk, shaking off as much excess buttermilk as possible. Roll fish pieces in the flour-crumb mixture, coating all sides. Shake off excess and carefully place fish, a few pieces at a time, into the hot oil, being careful not to crowd the pan. Lower heat to medium and cook, gently turning once or twice, until fish is deep brown, crispy and cooked through, about 5 to 7 minutes total. Remove fish to a rack set over paper towels to drain; sprinkle with salt while hot.

Serve halibut on a bed of coleslaw.

Serves 4

Main Courses

Curried Halibut

My friend Priya Keane and her mother, Peerooza, shared this recipe.

>   4 halibut steaks, about 8 ounces each
>   2 tablespoons fresh lemon juice
>   1 1/2 teaspoons salt, divided
>   1/2 teaspoon freshly ground pepper
>   1/4 cup vegetable oil
>   1/2 cup finely chopped onion
>   1/4 teaspoon ground hot red pepper (cayenne)
>   1/4 teaspoon turmeric
>   2 teaspoons ground coriander
>   3 medium tomatoes, chopped or 1 can (15 ounces) diced tomatoes
>   1/4 teaspoon garam masala (see **Note**)
>   4 tablespoons chopped fresh cilantro, divided

Preheat oven to 350°.

Wash the fish and pat dry with paper towels. Sprinkle both sides with lemon juice, 1 teaspoon of the salt and the black pepper and let stand at room temperature for 15 minutes.

In a heavy skillet, heat the oil over medium heat until a haze forms above it. Add the onions and cook until soft and golden brown, stirring often. Stir in remaining 1/2 teaspoon salt, cayenne, turmeric, and ground coriander, and cook for 30 seconds, then stir in the tomatoes and 2 tablespoons of cilantro. Cook for about 5 minutes. Place the fish in a baking dish. Spread the tomato mixture evenly on top of each piece, sprinkle with garam masala, cover with foil and bake fish for 30 minutes or until it flakes easily with a fork.

To serve, sprinkle the top with cilantro and enjoy.

Serves 4

Note: Garam masala, a mixture of ground spices commonly used in Indian cooking, is available in the spice section of most supermarkets.

Paprika Halibut with Green Olives

1 tablespoon olive oil
1 small red bell pepper, seeds removed, sliced about 1/4" thick
1 small onion, cut in half lengthwise and sliced about 1/4" thick
1/4 cup sliced pimento-stuffed green olives
2 teaspoons paprika
1/4 cup dry sherry, dry white wine, vermouth or water
3/4 pound to 1 pound halibut fillet, skin removed
Lemon juice
Salt and pepper

Preheat oven to 400°.

Heat olive oil over medium-high heat in a large skillet. Add bell pepper and onion and cook, stirring frequently, until vegetables are soft and onion is just beginning to brown, about 5 minutes. Remove from heat and add olives, paprika and sherry; stir to combine well.

Place halibut in a small, greased baking pan. Sprinkle top of fish with lemon juice, salt and pepper. Spoon bell pepper-onion mixture over halibut. Bake, uncovered, until fish is cooked through, 20 to 25 minutes (depending on thickness).

Serves 2

Main Courses

Marinated Halibut with Tzatziki

1 medium cucumber
1 cup plain (unflavored) Greek-style yogurt (see **Note**)
3 garlic cloves, minced or pressed, divided
3 tablespoons fresh lemon juice, divided
5 tablespoons olive oil, divided
3 teaspoons finely chopped fresh dill, divided
Salt to taste (optional)
1 teaspoon lemon zest (yellow part only)
1 1/2 to 2 pounds halibut fillets, cut into 4 portions

At least 2 hours or up to one day ahead, prepare the tzatziki: Peel the cucumber and cut in half lengthwise. Using a melon baller or small spoon, scoop seeds from the center and discard; finely chop the cucumber and place it in the center of a clean towel. Over the sink, twist the towel closed and squeeze as much liquid out of the cucumber as you can. In a bowl combine the cucumber, yogurt, 2 cloves of garlic, 1 tablespoon lemon juice, 1 tablespoon olive oil and 1 teaspoon of finely chopped dill. Cover and refrigerate at least 2 hours to develop flavors. Before serving, stir tzatziki and add salt if needed.

Preheat oven to 450°.

Combine remaining 2 tablespoons of lemon juice, 4 tablespoons olive oil, lemon zest, remaining 2 teaspoons chopped dill and 1 clove of garlic in a large zip-top bag. Add halibut, seal bag and turn to coat well with marinade. Let stand on counter for 15 to 20 minutes.

Remove halibut from marinade and arrange on a baking sheet lined with foil. Sprinkle top with salt if desired. Place in oven and bake 8 to 12 minutes (without turning), depending on thickness, until fish just flakes with a fork and is opaque in the center. Serve tzatziki on the side.

Serves 4

Note: Greek-style yogurt is thicker and has a higher protein content than regular yogurt. If you can't find it, you can substitute regular yogurt from which you have drained some of the liquid. To do this, place the yogurt in a strainer lined with paper towels and placed over a bowl. Refrigerate for 1 to 2 hours to let the liquid drain off.

Pistachio-Crusted Halibut

    Spicy Yogurt Sauce (recipe below)
    1/2 cup shelled and chopped pistachios
    2 tablespoons flour
    1/2 teaspoon salt
    1/4 teaspoon black pepper
    1 1/2 to 2 pounds halibut fillet, skin removed
    2 tablespoons olive oil, divided

Prepare Spicy Yogurt Sauce and refrigerate while you prepare the halibut.

Stir together pistachios, flour, salt and pepper in a shallow bowl or pie plate. Cut halibut into 4 serving-sized pieces and brush both sides with 1 tablespoon of the olive oil. Press halibut lightly into the pistachio-flour mixture.

Heat remaining oil in a large, non-stick skillet over medium-high heat. Add fish and cook until golden brown and just done, turning once, about 8 to 10 minutes total.

Serve fillets topped with a dollop of Spicy Yogurt Sauce; pass remaining sauce at the table.

Serves 4

Spicy Yogurt Sauce

    1 cup plain (unflavored) Greek-style yogurt (see **Note** on page 67)
    1/2 cucumber, peeled, seeded and finely diced
    1 tablespoon chopped fresh dill
    1 large clove garlic, minced or pressed
    1 tablespoon fresh lemon juice
    1 teaspoon paprika
    1 generous pinch red pepper flakes (add more or less to taste)
    1/2 teaspoon salt

Mix all ingredients in a small bowl. Refrigerate until ready to use.

Ray's Waterfront Halibut Andaman

Chef Leslie Simutis
Ray's Waterfront, Seward

Owner-chef Leslie Simutis took a trip in Thailand in the mid 1990s to study and learn the country's cuisine. The influence of that trip shows in this recipe; she named it "Halibut Andaman" after the Andaman Sea in Thailand. It is one of the restaurant's best-selling dishes.

- 2 1/2 teaspoons olive oil
- 1/2 tablespoon minced garlic
- 1/2 tablespoon curry powder
- 1/2 tablespoon Thai red curry paste
- 1/2 tablespoon ground coriander seed
- 2 3/4 tablespoons ketchup
- 1 1/2 tablespoons soy sauce
- 1 1/2 tablespoons brown sugar
- 3 cups unsweetened coconut milk (not "lite")
- 1 1/2 to 2 pounds halibut fillet
- Flour, seasoned with salt and pepper
- Egg wash (1 egg beaten with 1 tablespoon water)
- 1 1/2 cups crushed macadamia nuts

Preheat oven to 350°.

For sauce, blend olive oil, garlic, curry powder, curry paste, coriander, ketchup, soy sauce, brown sugar and coconut milk well in mixing bowl. Set sauce aside.

Cut halibut fillet into 4 serving-sized pieces. Dust halibut with seasoned flour and place on a lightly oiled baking sheet. Brush top of fish with egg wash and cover with crushed macadamia nuts. Bake halibut for 15 to 20 minutes depending on the thickness of the fillets (do not overcook or the fish will be dry).

Heat sauce in a saucepan to a simmer. Place baked halibut on serving plates and cover with sauce. Ray's serves this dish with cilantro lime rice and their vegetable of the day.

Serves 4

Quick Halibut and White Bean Casserole

> 2 cans (15 ounces each) cannellini or other white beans, drained and rinsed
> 1 to 1 1/2 pounds halibut steaks or skinless fillet, cut into 4 serving-sized pieces
> 1/2 cup dry white wine
> 3 tablespoons pesto, homemade (see **Note**) or purchased, divided
> 2 cloves garlic, minced or pressed
> 1/2 teaspoon salt
> 2 medium tomatoes, diced

Preheat oven to 375°.

Spray a baking pan or shallow casserole dish with non-stick cooking spray. Spoon beans into bottom of dish. Place halibut pieces on top of beans in a single layer; drizzle with wine then spread about half of the pesto evenly over the fish. In a small bowl, stir the remaining pesto, garlic and the salt into the tomatoes then spoon the mixture evenly over and around halibut.

Cover tightly with aluminum foil and bake 20 to 30 minutes (depending on thickness) or until fish is cooked through.

Serves 4

Note: The Green Sauce on page 91 works well with this recipe.

Main Courses

Simple Halibut Paprikash with Noodles

- 3/4 pound to 1 pound skinless halibut fillet, cut into 2 equal pieces
- 1 tablespoon butter
- 1 tablespoon olive oil
- 1/2 cup thinly sliced yellow onion
- 1 clove garlic, minced or pressed
- 1 to 3 teaspoons sweet paprika, preferably Hungarian (use more or less to taste)
- 1/2 cup chicken broth or water
- 1/4 teaspoon salt
- 1/2 cup sour cream (do not use fat-free)
- 4 ounces egg noodles, cooked according to package directions
- 1 tablespoon chopped parsley or fresh dill (for garnish)

Heat butter and oil in a medium sized, heavy skillet over medium-high heat. Add onions and cook, stirring, until soft. Stir in garlic and paprika and cook for 1 minute. Add broth and salt, stir to combine, then reduce heat to medium-low and add halibut. Cover and simmer until fish is just cooked through, about 6 to 8 minutes, depending on thickness.

Carefully remove cooked fish to a small plate and keep warm. Slowly whisk sour cream into the fish cooking liquid and onions and simmer for 2 to 3 minutes, stirring constantly until smooth. Once you've added the sour cream, do not allow the sauce to boil.

Place cooked noodles in a shallow serving bowl. Place fish on top of noodles; pour sauce over fish, sprinkle with parsley or dill and serve.

Serves 2

Roast Alaska Halibut with Fennel and Cannellini Beans

This recipe is used by permission of Alaska Seafood Marketing Institute, www.alaskaseafood.org.

>   4 wild Alaska halibut fillets, abut 6 ounces each
>   Juice of 1 lemon
>   Finely grated rind (yellow part only) from 1 lemon
>   Salt and freshly ground black pepper
>   2 tablespoons butter, melted
>   1 tablespoon olive oil
>   1 bulb fennel, finely sliced
>   2 cans (14 ounces each) cannellini beans, drained and rinsed
>   1 teaspoon vegetable stock powder or 1/2 a vegetable stock cube
>   2 tablespoons capers
>   2 tablespoons roughly chopped flat-leaf parsley

Preheat a grill to medium-high. Cover the grill rack with foil and arrange the halibut fillets on top (or place them on a greased baking sheet). Sprinkle with half the lemon juice, season with salt and pepper and drizzle with half the butter. Grill for 6 to 8 minutes, turning once.

Meanwhile, heat the remaining butter with the olive oil in a large frying pan. Add the sliced fennel and cook it for 2 to 3 minutes, until softened and beginning to brown.

Add the cannellini beans to the pan with the fennel. Stir in the lemon rind, remaining lemon juice, the stock powder or cube and a splash of hot water. Cook over medium-high heat, stirring occasionally, for 4 to 5 minutes.

Divide the bean mixture among four warmed plates or shallow bowls. Arrange the halibut fillets on top, then scatter the capers and parsley over the fish. Serve immediately.

Serves 4

Main Courses

Quick Halibut with Corn and Tomatoes

    2 tablespoons vegetable oil, divided
    1/2 cup diced sweet onion (such as Vidalia or Walla Walla)
    1 large clove garlic, minced or pressed
    2 cups cherry or grape tomatoes, halved
    2 cups fresh or frozen corn kernels
    1 teaspoon fresh thyme leaves (or 1/2 teaspoon dried thyme)
    2 tablespoons balsamic vinegar
    1 1/2 to 2 pounds halibut fillet, skin removed
    Salt and pepper
    2 tablespoons cornmeal
    1 tablespoon chopped cilantro or flat-leaf parsley

Heat 1 tablespoon vegetable oil in a large skillet over medium-high heat. Add onions and cook, stirring often, until they just begin to soften. Add garlic, tomatoes, corn and thyme; stir and continue to cook for about 5 minutes. Stir in balsamic vinegar. Remove vegetables to a bowl and keep warm.

Wipe out skillet, add remaining tablespoon of oil and return to medium-high heat. Cut halibut into 4 serving pieces. Season fish on both sides with salt and pepper, then coat lightly with the cornmeal. Place halibut in pan and reduce heat to medium. Cook until fish is just done, turning once, about 8 to 12 minutes total, depending on thickness.

Spoon vegetables on top of the cooked halibut, sprinkle with cilantro, and serve.

Serves 4

Roasted Halibut with Tomatoes and Olives

>1 1/2 to 2 pounds skinless halibut fillets, cut into 4 equal portions
>1 tablespoon butter, softened
>Salt and pepper
>1/4 cup olive oil
>1 tablespoon balsamic or red-wine vinegar
>1 small clove garlic, minced or pressed
>2 cups grape or cherry tomatoes, cut in half (or quartered if tomatoes are very large)
>1/2 cup pitted olives, preferably Kalamata, cut into halves
>1/4 cup very thinly sliced red onion
>1/4 cup fresh basil leaves, cut crosswise into thin ribbons
>Whole basil leaves for garnish (optional)

Preheat oven to 425°.

Place halibut pieces in a greased baking pan. Pat the fish dry with a paper towel, then rub tops of pieces with softened butter. Season to taste with salt and pepper. Bake fish for 10 to 12 minutes or until it is opaque and flakes easily with a fork.

While the fish is baking, combine the olive oil, vinegar, garlic and salt and pepper to taste in the bottom of a medium bowl. Whisk to mix well. Add tomatoes, olives, red onion and basil and toss gently to coat with dressing. Set aside at room temperature.

To serve, place halibut on plates and spoon tomato-olive mixture on top and around fillets. Garnish with whole basil leaves, if desired.

Serves 4

Main Courses

Zesty Halibut and Pasta

>3 tablespoons olive oil
>1 medium yellow onion, chopped
>2 large cloves garlic, minced or pressed
>1 can (14 ounces) diced tomatoes
>1/2 cup dry white or red wine or water
>1 teaspoon dried oregano
>1/2 teaspoon sugar
>1/2 teaspoon salt
>1/4 teaspoon black pepper
>1 pinch red pepper flakes (or more to taste)
>1 to 1 1/2 pounds skinless halibut fillet, cut into 4 serving pieces
>1/2 cup pitted olives, preferable Kalamata, halved
>1/2 pound linguine or fettucine, cooked according to package directions
>Grated Parmesan cheese (for serving)

In a large skillet with cover, heat olive oil over medium-high heat. Add onion and cook, stirring occasionally, until soft (about 5 minutes). Stir in garlic and cook 1 more minute. Add tomatoes, wine, oregano, sugar, salt, black pepper and red pepper flakes. Mix well, reduce heat to medium and cover and cook for 5 minutes.

Remove cover and place halibut pieces into tomato sauce, spooning some of the sauce over the top of the fillets. Cover pan and cook until halibut is done, about 8 to 10 minutes.

Pile cooked pasta into a serving bowl; spoon on about half the sauce from the pan and toss it with the pasta. Top with the halibut pieces then pour the remaining sauce over all. Serve with Parmesan cheese.

Serves 4

African-Style Halibut and Pumpkin Casserole

1/4 cup vegetable oil
1 large onion, diced
Pinch of red pepper flakes (use more or less, to taste)
2 teaspoons cumin
1/2 teaspoon nutmeg
2 large tomatoes, seeded and diced
1 teaspoon salt
1/2 teaspoon black pepper
3 cups pumpkin or other winter squash (Butternut, Hubbard, etc.), peeled, seeded and cut into 1" cubes
1 pound skinless halibut fillet
1 1/2 cups white rice, uncooked
4 cups vegetable or chicken broth

Preheat oven to 350°.

In a medium-sized Dutch oven or deep casserole dish with tight-fitting lid, heat oil over medium-high heat. Add onion, red pepper flakes, cumin and nutmeg and cook, stirring often, until onions are soft and just beginning to brown. Remove from heat.

Scatter tomatoes over onions, sprinkle with half the salt and pepper, then add the pumpkin cubes in one layer. Press gently to level ingredients in pot. Cut halibut into pieces to fit, then place fish on top of pumpkin in an even layer and sprinkle with remaining salt and pepper. Pour rice evenly over the top, then carefully pour broth over all.

Cover tightly (use foil if lid is not tight) and bake for 30 minutes or until pumpkin is tender and rice is cooked. Remove from oven and let casserole stand, covered, for 10 to 15 minutes before serving.

Serves 4

Main Courses

Mediterranean Halibut with Eggplant and Zucchini

    2 tablespoons olive oil, divided
    1 small Japanese eggplant, cut into 1/2" cubes
    1 small zucchini, cut into 1/2" cubes
    2 scallions, thinly sliced
    1 large clove garlic, minced or pressed
    1 large tomato, peeled (if desired), seeded and diced
    1 small can (2.25 ounces) sliced black olives, drained
    1/4 teaspoon dried oregano
    1/4 teaspoon red pepper flakes (use more or less, to taste)
    1 tablespoon balsamic vinegar
    Salt and pepper
    1/2 to 3/4 pound halibut fillet, cut into 2 portions
    Grated or shredded Parmesan cheese (for serving)

Heat 1 tablespoon olive oil in a large skillet over medium-high heat. Add eggplant, zucchini and 2 tablespoons water and cook, stirring often, until vegetables soften, about 5 minutes. Stir in scallions and garlic and continue cooking another 1 to 2 minutes. Add tomato, olives, oregano, red pepper flakes and balsamic vinegar. Stir to combine well, reduce heat to medium-low and push vegetables to the sides of the pan.

Spoon remaining tablespoon of olive oil into the center of the skillet to heat. Season halibut pieces with salt and pepper and place, skin side down, into the skillet. Cover and cook until halibut is almost done, about 6 to 9 minutes, depending on thickness.

Spoon vegetables evenly over halibut pieces and serve, passing the Parmesan cheese at the table.

Serves 2

Kinley's Almond-Crusted Halibut with Cider-Cherry Beurre Blanc

Chef Brett Knipmeyer
Kinley's Restaurant, Anchorage

Almond-Crusted Halibut

    1 1/2 pounds halibut fillet, cut into 4 portions about 6 ounces each
    Sea salt and freshly ground pepper
    1 cup all-purpose flour
    1 egg
    1 cup milk
    1/2 cup water
    2/3 cup Panko (Japanese bread crumbs)
    2/3 cup sliced almonds, lightly toasted
    Canola oil (for frying)
    Cider-Cherry Beurre Blanc (recipe on opposite page)

To prepare the halibut, season fillets with salt and pepper. Place the flour in a shallow bowl. In another shallow bowl or pie plate, combine the egg, milk and water. In a food processor, pulse Panko and almonds until mixture is the consistency of coarse meal; transfer to a plate. Dredge fillets in flour, dip in egg mixture, then press into the Panko-almond mixture. Set fillets aside.

In a large skillet, add enough canola oil to come halfway up the thickest part of the fillets; heat the oil over medium-high heat until it shimmers. Add fillets in single layer and cook until golden; flip, cook until other side is golden and just done, about 6 minutes total. Drain on paper towels and keep warm.

To serve, divide the beurre blanc among 4 warm plates. Top with halibut and garnish each fillet with 4 cherries from the sauce.

Serves 4

Cider-Cherry Beurre Blanc

2 cans (15-ounces each) dark sweet cherries
1 1/2 cups fresh or organic apple cider
1/2 cup white wine
1 tablespoon minced shallot
1/2 cup heavy cream
1/2 cup (1 stick) unsalted butter, cut into pieces
Sea salt

Pour off juice from cherries (you should have about 1 1/2 cups). In a large saucepan simmer the cherry juice, cider, wine, shallot and cream until reduced to about 1/2 cup. Strain into another saucepan. Remove from heat and whisk in the butter piece by piece until just melted. Add the cherries and season to taste with salt. Keep warm, but do not reheat.

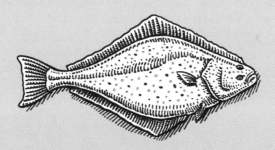

Halibut with Herb Yogurt

1 pound skinless halibut fillet, about 1" thick
1/4 teaspoon salt
1/8 teaspoon black pepper
1/2 cup plain, unflavored yogurt (not fat free)
2 teaspoons finely chopped fresh tarragon (see **Note**)
1 tablespoon finely chopped fresh parsley

Preheat oven to 400°F.

Pat fillet dry with a paper towel, then cut into 2 equal portions and season with salt and pepper. Place fish in a shallow, greased baking dish.

In a small bowl, mix yogurt, the tarragon and about half of the parsley. Spread the mixture evenly over the top of the fillets. Place fish in oven and bake 12 to 15 minutes, until it is cooked through. Sprinkle with remaining parsley and serve.

Serves 2

Note: Try substituting other fresh herbs such as thyme, basil, dill, rosemary or chives for the tarragon.

Halibut Croquettes

    1 large baking potato
    2 tablespoons butter, softened to room temperature
    1/2 cup milk
    1/2 teaspoon salt
    1/4 teaspoon black pepper
    Pinch of cayenne (more if desired)
    2 tablespoons finely chopped chives
    3/4 pound to 1 pound cooked halibut (skin removed), broken into pieces
    2 eggs
    1/2 cup all-purpose flour, seasoned with salt and pepper
    1 to 2 cups bread crumbs (Panko, Japanese-style bread crumbs, or homemade crumbs work best in this recipe)
    1 cup vegetable oil, for frying

Peel potato and cut into 1" chunks. Place in a saucepan, cover with water and boil over medium high heat until fork tender. Drain potatoes then mash with butter and milk until creamy. Add salt, pepper and chives, then gently stir in halibut until well combined. Let stand until cool enough to handle, then form mixture into golf ball-sized balls and flatten them slightly to about 1" thick.

Beat the eggs in a shallow bowl. Place flour and bread crumbs in two other bowls. Dip croquettes first into flour, then into egg, then bread crumbs.

Heat the oil in a large, deep frying pan over medium-high heat. Gently place croquettes into oil and fry several at a time (do not crowd pan) until golden brown, turning as needed. Remove and drain on paper towels before serving.

Serves 4

Halibut en Baguette

The inspiration for this recipe was Joanne Weir's "Pork Roasted the Way the Tuscans Do," a pork tenderloin roasted in a baguette. You can find her original recipe at www.joanneweir.com.

>   1 piece of crusty baguette, *bâtarde* or other narrow French bread loaf, about 4" wide and 8" to 10" long
>   3 tablespoons olive oil
>   4 tablespoons Green Sauce (see recipe on page 91)
>   3/4 pound to 1 pound skinless halibut fillet
>   Salt and pepper

Preheat oven to 375°.

Cut a long slit lengthwise along the top of the bread. Do not cut all the way through. Gently pull the slit open then, using your fingers, pull out some of the soft bread from both sides, leaving a shell at least 1/2" all around.

In a small bowl, combine the olive oil and Green Sauce. Generously brush mixture over the inside of the bread. Top with the halibut fillet, cut in pieces to fit snugly into the cavity in the bread. Season fish with salt and pepper and brush the remaining Green Sauce mixture on top of it.

Tie the bread closed at each end and in the middle with kitchen string, making sure that the fish is completely enclosed by the bread.

Place bread on a baking sheet and bake for 25 to 35 minutes, until an instant-read thermometer inserted into the middle of the halibut registers 130° to 135°. Remove from oven and let rest at least 10 minutes (fish will continue to cook as it stands).

Cut into 1" to 2" slices with a serrated knife and serve.

Serves 2 to 3

Main Courses

Halibut Salad Sandwiches

2 cups cooked halibut (about 1 pound), skin and bones removed
1/4 cup chopped celery
1/4 cup red or yellow onion, finely diced
3 tablespoons capers, drained and roughly chopped (or substitute 3 tablespoons chopped green olives)
1/2 cup mayonnaise, bottled or homemade (recipe on page 88)
1 teaspoon Dijon mustard
Salt and pepper to taste
4 soft sandwich rolls or 8 slices bread, buttered and/or toasted if desired
4 lettuce leaves
4 large slices tomato

Use leftover halibut or steam or poach fish according to basic instructions on page 34. Chill cooked fish before proceeding with recipe.

In a medium bowl, combine halibut, celery, onions, capers, mayonnaise, mustard and salt and pepper. Stir to mix well, adding more mayonnaise if mixture is too dry.

Spread halibut salad on rolls or bread, top with lettuce and tomato if using, and serve.

Makes 4 sandwiches

Skillet Barbequed Halibut Burgers

1 pound skinless halibut fillet, cut into 1" chunks
1/4 cup onion, finely diced
2 tablespoons vegetable oil, divided
3 tablespoons bottled barbeque sauce (plus more for serving)
1/4 cup dry bread crumbs
Salt and pepper to taste
1 large tomato, sliced
1 cup shredded lettuce
4 large hamburger buns or Kaiser rolls, split and toasted if desired

Place halibut chunks in the work bowl of food processor. Pulse several times or until halibut is well chopped but not puréed (or you can chop the halibut by hand into cubes no larger than 1/4"). Place chopped fish in a bowl; add onion, 1 tablespoon vegetable oil and barbeque sauce. Gently mix until all ingredients are evenly distributed. Form mixture into 4 patties and place on a sheet of waxed paper or foil. Refrigerate for 20 to 30 minutes.

Heat remaining tablespoon of vegetable oil in a large skillet over medium-high heat. Spread bread crumbs on a plate and season with salt and pepper. Dip chilled halibut burgers into crumbs, pressing crumbs into both sides. Carefully place burgers into skillet, reduce heat to medium and cook, turning once, until cooked through (about 8 to 10 minutes total).

Serve cooked halibut burgers on buns with sliced tomato, shredded lettuce and additional barbeque sauce if desired.

Serves 4

Main Courses

Smoked Halibut Club Sandwiches

Less common than its ubiquitous relative, smoked salmon, smoked halibut is a treat worth looking for. This recipe susbstitutes smoked halibut for the bacon in a classic double-decker club sandwich.

>   6 slices good quality white bread, toasted
>   Classic Tartar Sauce (see recipe on page 89)
>   3 to 4 ounces smoked halibut, sliced or broken into small pieces
>   3 to 4 ounces sliced turkey
>   2 hard-boiled eggs, sliced (optional)
>   4 leaves Romaine lettuce
>   1 large ripe tomato, cut into 4 thick slices

Spread 2 slices of toasted bread with about 1 tablespoon of tartar sauce. Top each with a tomato slice, half the smoked halibut and a lettuce leaf (cut to fit). Place a second slice of bread on top of each lettuce leaf. Spread these slices of bread with another tablespoon of tartar sauce, then top each one with half the turkey, half the egg slices, a slice of tomato and a lettuce leaf.

Spread the last 2 slices of bread with about 1 tablespoon of tartar sauce. Place the bread, sauce side down, on top of the sandwiches. Cut sandwiches in half and secure with frilled toothpicks if desired.

Serves 2

Sauces, Marinades & Embellishments

Moroccan Chermoula Sauce and Marinade

Chermoula is a zesty concoction made with herbs and spices and traditionally served with fish. Marinate the fish for 20 to 30 minutes before broiling or grilling, or serve the Chermoula as a sauce spooned over grilled or baked fish.

- 1 cup finely chopped cilantro or flat-leaf parsley or combination of both
- 3 cloves garlic, minced or pressed
- 1 tablespoon sweet paprika
- 1 tablespoon ground cumin
- 1/2 teaspoon salt
- 1/8 teaspoon cayenne or crushed red pepper flakes (more or less to taste)
- 2 tablespoons lemon juice
- 1/3 cup (or more) olive oil

Combine all ingredients in a bowl and stir to mix well. Add more olive oil if needed to achieve the desired consistency (Chermoula should be fairly thick).

Makes about 1 cup

Homemade Mayonnaise

Although making your own mayonnaise sounds intimidating, if you have a blender it is quick and easy.

> 1 egg yolk, at room temperature (see **Note**)
> 1/2 teaspoon salt
> 1/2 teaspoon dry mustard
> 2 teaspoons white wine vinegar
> 1 tablespoon fresh squeezed lemon juice
> 1 cup mild-tasting oil, such as canola, safflower or light or extra-light olive oil

Place egg yolk, salt, dry mustard, vinegar and lemon juice in blender. Blend for about 15 seconds on low speed. Leave the motor running and slowly pour in the oil, a few drops at a time. Stop occasionally to scrape the sides of the blender. Once the mayonnaise lightens in color and starts to thicken you can increase the flow of oil to a small, steady stream until it is all incorporated. If the mixture is too thick, thin it with a small amount (1 teaspoon at a time) of hot water. Cover tightly and refrigerate for up to 1 week.

Makes about 1 cup

Note: If you are reluctant to eat raw eggs because of the risk of salmonella or other food-borne illness, use pasteurized eggs.

Aïoli (Garlic Mayonnaise)

Prepare Homemade Mayonnaise as instructed above except begin by adding 3 cloves of garlic, minced or pressed, with the egg yolk. Proceed with recipe as given. Cover tightly and refrigerate for up to 1 week.

Makes about 1 cup

Sauces, Marinades & Embellishments

Classic Tartar Sauce

This is truly the classic sauce to serve with any fish, from frozen fish sticks to mahi-mahi. Variations to the classic recipe abound, with embellishments such as chopped dill or parsley, sweet pickle or chopped hard-boiled egg. Tadich Grill, a San Francisco institution, is famous for their tartar sauce made with the addition of mashed potatoes.

    3/4 cup mayonnaise, bottled or homemade (recipe on facing page)
    1 teaspoon Dijon mustard
    2 tablespoons chopped dill pickle or chopped capers
    1 tablespoon finely chopped scallion (optional)

Combine all ingredients in a small bowl. Refrigerate until needed.

Makes about 1 cup

Remoulade Sauce

Remoulade is a classic French sauce used with fish and shellfish or as a dressing on seafood salads.

    1 cup mayonnaise, bottled or homemade (recipe on facing page)
    1 tablespoon minced capers
    1 tablespoon minced gherkins or other sour pickles
    2 teaspoons Dijon mustard
    1 teaspoon anchovy paste
    1 teaspoon finely chopped parsley
    1 teaspoon finely chopped tarragon or chervil or combination

Combine all ingredients in a small bowl. Refrigerate until needed.

Makes about 1 cup

Rouille (Red-Chili Mayonnaise)

Rouille, a spicy cousin of mayonnaise that is an integral part of classic French Bouillabaisse, *is also often served with other fish and fish stews.*

>   3 tablespoons warm water
>   3/4 cup stale French bread, cut or torn into coarse crumbs
>   2 cloves garlic, coarsely chopped
>   1/2 teaspoon salt
>   Pinch of saffron
>   1/2 teaspoon cayenne (more or less to taste)
>   1/3 cup olive oil

In a small bowl, pour warm water over bread crumbs; let stand 15 to 20 minutes or until water is absorbed and bread is soft.

In a blender, pulse the softened bread crumbs with the garlic, salt, saffron and cayenne until combined into a smooth paste. With the motor running, add the olive oil in a slow stream and blend until the sauce is smooth.

Makes about 1 cup

Lemon-Garlic Butter

>   3 tablespoons butter
>   1 tablespoon finely minced shallot
>   2 tablespoons lemon juice

Melt butter over medium heat. Add shallot and cook, stirring, for about 2 minutes, until soft. Raise heat to high, whisk in lemon juice and pour immediately over broiled, grilled or pan-fried halibut.

Makes about 1/3 cup

Sauces, Marinades & Embellishments

Basic Chimichurri

Chimichurri is popular in South America, where it is used as both a marinade and sauce for meat, chicken and fish.

- 1/2 cup coarsely chopped, packed flat leaf parsley
- 3 cloves of garlic, coarsely chopped
- 1/4 cup red wine vinegar
- 1/2 teaspoon salt
- 1/2 teaspoon red pepper flakes (more or less to taste)
- 1/2 teaspoon freshly ground black pepper
- 1/2 cup extra virgin olive oil

Place all ingredients except the olive oil in a food processor and process until puréed. Transfer to a bowl, pour olive oil over the top and let stand at room temperature for an hour or two. Stir before using. Chimichurri is best the day it is made but can be stored in the refrigerator for 2 to 3 days. Bring to room temperature before using.

Makes about 1 cup

Green Sauce

Great on fish, this sauce can also be used in any recipe calling for pesto.

- 1 cup chopped cilantro
- 1 cup chopped basil
- 1/2 cup chopped flat-leaf parsley
- 4 garlic cloves, coarsely chopped
- 2 teaspoons lemon zest
- 1 teaspon salt
- 1/2 teaspoon ground pepper
- 2 tablespoons lemon juice
- 1 cup extra virgin olive oil

Place all ingredients in food processor; process until well combined.

Makes about 2 cups

Compound Butters

Compound butter, a mixture of butter and one or more herb or other item, is great to have on hand for a variety of uses. A pat of this rich, aromatic butter melting over a piece of fresh, perfectly-steamed or poached halibut makes a simple but impressive meal.

>1/2 cup butter (1 stick), at room temperature
>Herbs or ginger as specified in the recipes below

Combine ingredients as instructed in the specific recipe below. Spoon butter onto waxed paper or plastic wrap and roll into a log about 4" long. Twist ends and refrigerate at least an hour or until ready to use, up to 2 days. For longer storage, compound butters can be frozen for up to 1 month. To serve, slice into 1/2" disks and place on top of hot fish. Makes 8 servings.

Herb Butter

>1/2 cup (1 stick) butter, at room temperature
>2 tablespoons finely minced fresh herbs, such as tarragon, dill, chives or chervil

Thoroughly combine softened butter and one or more of the listed herbs. Wrap and store as detailed above.

Ginger Butter

>1/2 cup (1 stick) butter, at room temperature
>1 tablespoon fresh ginger, finely grated

Melt about 2 tablespoons of the butter in a small microwave-safe bowl or small saucepan. Stir in the ginger; set aside and let steep for about 20 to 30 minutes, stirring occasionally. Pour ginger and butter mixture (rewarm if butter has solidified) into a fine mesh strainer and strain the liquid into the remaining butter. Push on the ginger with the back of a spoon to remove all the liquid. Mix well. Wrap and store as detailed above.

Romesco Sauce

Romesco is a flavorful sauce from Spain that makes a perfect accompaniment to grilled or broiled fish.

    3 medium vine-ripened tomatoes
    1 red bell pepper
    6 cloves garlic, peeled
    1/2 cup almonds
    3/4 cup plus 1 tablespoon olive oil
    1 slice stale bread
    1/2 cup red wine vinegar
    1 teaspoon sweet paprika
    Pinch red pepper flakes (more or less to taste)
    1 teaspoon salt

Preheat oven to 450°.

Cut tomatoes in half; squeeze out seeds and juice. Cut red pepper in half and remove core and seeds. Place tomatoes and pepper on a rimmed baking sheet with garlic cloves and almonds. Drizzle with 1 tablespoon olive oil. Bake 10 minutes, stirring once or twice.

Cool vegetables and almonds for about 10 minutes, then place them (and any juices accumulated in the pan) into the work bowl of a food processor. Add bread, torn into small pieces, vinegar, paprika, red pepper flakes and salt. Process until smooth then, with motor running, drizzle in olive oil in a steady stream until all is incorporated.

Allow sauce to stand at room temperature at least an hour for flavors to develop, then stir and adjust salt and red pepper flakes to taste. Leftover sauce can be covered and refrigerated for several days or frozen for 1 to 2 months.

Makes about 2 cups

Recipe Index

African-Style Halibut and Pumpkin Casserole 76
Aïoli (Garlic Mayonnaise)...88
Asian Halibut Stir-Fry...51
Bacon-Wrapped Halibut Pops...11
Baked Halibut Fillets..36
Baked Halibut with Bread Crumb Topping 35
Baked Halibut with Vermouth 38
Basic Chimichurri..91
Basic Oven-Roasted Halibut 33
Basic Poached Halibut..34
Basic Steamed Halibut..34
Blackberry Vinaigrette 45
Buttermilk Fried Halibut with Spicy Slaw 64
Classic Tartar Sauce 89
Compound Butters 92
Crab-Stuffed Halibut Cheeks 59
Creamy Avocado Sauce 57
Curried Halibut 65
Double Musky Halibut Ceviche...20
Easy Halibut Posole 25
Ginger Butter 92
Glacier Brewhouse Halibut with
    Raspberry-Roasted Shallot Butter................................44
Green Sauce...91
Halibut à L'Orange...39
Halibut Amandine..40
Halibut and Avocado Salad 18
Halibut and Shiitake Packets..50
Halibut Caddy Ganty..41
Halibut Cheeks with Bacon and Shallot Relish......................58
Halibut Chowder...23
Halibut Cocktail Kebabs 12
Halibut Croquettes 81
Halibut en Baguette 82
Halibut Fajitas...62
Halibut Gratin...46
Halibut Nacho Bites 13
Halibut Olympia..47
Halibut Poached in Cream 42
Halibut Pot Pie 48

Recipe Index

Halibut Salad Sandwiches 83
Halibut with Creamy Mushroom Sauce 43
Halibut with Herb Yogurt 80
Halibut with Mango, Red Pepper and Tomato Salsa 63
Halibut, Couscous and Zucchini Stew 30
Halibut, Squash and Ginger Soup 31
Herb Butter 92
Homemade Mayonnaise 88
Homer Wahoo Halibut Tacos 56
Homestead Halibut with Sweet Pea and Lemon Risotto 53
Hot and Sour Halibut Soup 26
Island Style Halibut Salad 17
Jens' Halibut Menunière à la Bonne Femme 60
Kinley's Almond-Crusted Halibut with
    Cider-Cherry Beurre Blanc 78
Korean Halibut with Bok Choy and Eggplant 54
Lemon-Garlic Butter 90
Ludvig's Thai Halibut Soup 27
Marinated Halibut with Tzatziki 67
Mediterranean Halibut Soup 29
Mediterranean Halibut with Eggplant and Zucchini 77
Mini Halibut Cakes 14
Moroccan Chermoula Sauce and Marinade 87
Pan-Seared Halibut with Sesame-Ginger Vinaigrette 55
Paprika Halibut with Green Olives 66
Paradiso's Baked Halibut 37
Pickled Halibut 16
Pistachio Crusted Halibut 68
Quick Halibut and White Bean Casserole 70
Quick Halibut with Fresh Corn and Tomatoes 73
Raspberry-Roasted Shallot Butter 44
Ray's Waterfront Halibut Andaman 69
Remoulade Sauce 89
Roast Alaska Halibut with Fennel and Cannellini Beans 72
Roasted Halibut with Tomatoes and Olives 74
Romesco Sauce 93
Rouille (Red-Chili Mayonnaise) 90
Simple Halibut Paprikash with Noodles 71
Skillet Barbequed Halibut Burgers 84
Smoked Halibut Club Sandwiches 85
Stir-Fried Halibut with Mushrooms and Asparagus 52
Stuffed Halibut Fillets 49
Tropical Halibut and Black Bean Salad 19
Vietnamese Halibut Soup 28
Wasabi's Hot-Butt Dip 15
White Halibut Chili 24
Zesty Halibut and Pasta 75

Two More Excellent Alaska Cookbooks!

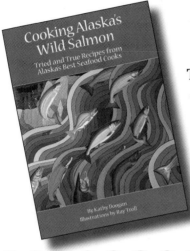

Alaska's Classic Salmon Cookbook

These tried and true recipes from Alaska's best seafood chefs take advantage of the abundance of wild salmon available in Alaska's pristine, icy cold waters.

To order send US$19.95 (incudes US$6.00 postage & handling) to the address listed below.

Not Just Alaska's Best Selling Cookbook, But Alaska's Best Selling Book!

Best of the Best from Alaska Cookbook is a comprehensive collection of Alaska's most popular recipes from 56 classic Alaska cookbooks that capture Alaska's cuisine.

To order send US$22.95 (includes US$6.00 postage & handling) to the address listed below.

Order Both
Makes Great Gifts

Todd Communications
611 E. 12th Ave., Suite 102 • Anchorage, Alaska • 99501-4603 U.S.A.
Telephone: (907) 274-TODD (8633) • Telefax: (907) 929-5550
Sales@toddcom.com • WWW.ALASKABOOKSANDCALENDARS.COM
With other offices and warehouses in:
Ketchikan, Juneau, Fairbanks and Nome, Alaska